FastTrack
MUSIC INSTRUCTION

Chords & Scales
for Ukulele

Johnson

PLAYBACK+
Speed • Pitch • Balance • Loop

To access audio visit:
www.halleonard.com/mylibrary

Enter Code
4931-3354-5066-1531

ISBN 978-1-5400-3626-1

Visit Hal Leonard Online at
www.halleonard.com

Contact us:
Hal Leonard
7777 West Bluemound Road
Milwaukee, WI 53213
Email: info@halleonard.com

In Europe, contact:
Hal Leonard Europe Limited
42 Wigmore Street
Marylebone, London, W1U 2RN
Email: info@halleonardeurope.com

In Australia, contact:
Hal Leonard Australia Pty. Ltd.
4 Lentara Court
Cheltenham, Victoria, 3192 Australia
Email: info@halleonard.com.au

INTRODUCTION

Why you bought this book...

Hello again. We say "again" because we're assuming that you've already been through **FastTrack Ukulele 1** and **2**. (At the very least, **Book 1**.) If so—terrific! You've decided to keep learning your instrument, and you're ready for this supplemental book.

This book provides five important things:

 Basic chord theory

 Easy-find index of over 1,500 different ukulele chords and voicings

 Basic scale and mode theory

 Patterns for eight scales and seven modes

5 Special "Jam Session" using the chords and scales introduced

IMPORTANT: This book is a reference book (much like a dictionary) and should not take the place of a ukulele instruction book. That being said, please go through **FastTrack Ukulele 1** and **2** (or at least act like it, so we'll stop nagging).

Remember, if your fingers hurt, take a break. Many of these chords and scales will likely be unfamiliar and awkward at first. With practice and patience, though, you can learn them all.

So, when you're ready, tune up, crack your knuckles, and let's learn some chords and scales...

ABOUT THE AUDIO

Glad you noticed the added bonus—audio! Each of the tracks in the special "Jam Session" are included, so you can hear how it sounds and play along. Take a listen whenever you see this symbol:

WHERE TO FIND THINGS

LET'S DIVE RIGHT IN

What's a chord?

A chord is defined as three or more notes played at the same time. Chords provide the **harmony** that supports the melody of a song.

Sometimes chords are indicated by **chord symbols**, written (usually) above the musical staff. A chord symbol is simply an abbreviation for the name of that chord. For example, the symbol for an **F-sharp minor seven** chord would be **F♯m7**.

Get organized...

A chord symbol tells us two things about the chord—**root** and **type**:

1. The **root** gives the chord its name. For example, the root of a C chord is the note C. However, the root note is not always at the bottom of the chord. Notice the difference in txhese two types of C chords:

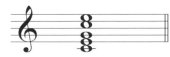   

C major with C on bottom   C minor with G on bottom

2. The chord's **type** is indicated by a **suffix** (m, 7, sus, maj9). There are lots of chord types and suffixes, but there's no need to panic—with a little practice, they're easy to recognize. This book groups all the chords by their type, so keep this list handy:

Suffix	Chord Type	Suffix	Chord Type
no suffix	major	maj7, M7	major seventh
m, min, -	minor	m7, min7, -7	minor seventh
+, aug, ♯5	augmented	m(maj7), m(+7)	minor, major seventh
°, dim, ♭5	diminished	maj7♭5, maj7(-5)	major seventh, flat fifth
sus4, sus	suspended fourth	m7♭5, m7(-5)	minor seventh, flat fifth
sus2, sus	suspended second	7♯5, +7	augmented seventh
add9	added ninth	7♭5, 7(-5)	seventh, flat fifth
m(add9)	minor added ninth	7♭9, 7(-9)	seventh, flat ninth
5, (no3)	fifth (a.k.a. "power chord")	7♯9, 7(♯9)	seventh, sharp ninth
6	sixth	+7♭9	augmented seventh, flat ninth
m6, -6	minor sixth	9	ninth
6/9	sixth, added ninth	maj9, M9	major ninth
m6/9	minor sixth, added ninth	m9, min9	minor ninth
7, dom7	seventh	11	eleventh
°7, dim7, dim	diminished seventh	m11, min11	minor eleventh
7sus4, 7sus	seventh, suspended fourth	13	thirteenth

Of course, you may run across other types of chords from time to time, but the ones listed above are the most common.

BUILDING CHORDS

Chords are built from simple "building blocks" called **intervals.** An interval is the distance between any two notes. Here's a look at the basic intervals, using C as a root:

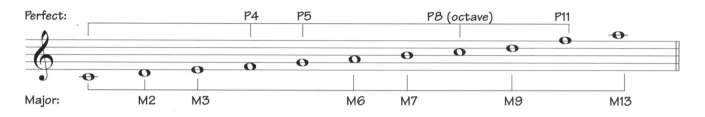

Notice that these intervals are divided into two groups—**major (M)** and **perfect (P)**. EASY TO REMEMBER: fourths, fifths, octaves, and elevenths are perfect; all other intervals are major.

Everything's relative...

Intervals come in many shapes and sizes, but in only five categories: **major, minor, perfect, augmented,** and **diminished.**

Here's how the categories are related:

A **major** interval lowered
one half step equals a **minor** interval.

A **major** or **perfect** interval raised
one half step equals an **augmented** interval.

A **perfect** interval lowered
one half step equals a **diminished** interval.

An interval's **type** is determined by the number of **steps** between the two notes.

☞ HELPFUL REMINDER: On your ukulele, from one fret to the next equals one half step; two frets apart equals one whole step.

Review the following chart and get to know all of the interval types...

Interval	Abbreviation	Steps	Pitches	Interval	Abbreviation	Steps	Pitches
unison	unis	none	*(notation)*	major sixth	M6	4 1/2	*(notation)*
minor second	m2	half	*(notation)*	augmented sixth*	aug6	5	*(notation)*
major second	M2	whole	*(notation)*	minor seventh*	m7	5	*(notation)*
augmented second*	aug2	1 1/2	*(notation)*	major seventh	M7	5 1/2	*(notation)*
minor third *	m3	1 1/2	*(notation)*	perfect octave	P8	6	*(notation)*
major third	M3	2	*(notation)*	minor ninth	m9	6 1/2	*(notation)*
perfect fourth	P4	2 1/2	*(notation)*	major ninth	M9	7	*(notation)*
augmented fourth*	aug4	3	*(notation)*	augmented ninth	aug9	7 1/2	*(notation)*
diminished fifth*	dim5	3	*(notation)*	perfect eleventh	P11	8 1/2	*(notation)*
perfect fifth	P5	3 1/2	*(notation)*	augmented eleventh	aug11	9	*(notation)*
augmented fifth*	aug5	4	*(notation)*	minor thirteenth	m13	10 1/2	*(notation)*
minor sixth*	m6	4	*(notation)*	major thirteenth	M13	11	*(notation)*

* NOTE: As with sharps and flats, some intervals may sound the same but are written two ways (for example, aug4 and dim5). Notes or intervals that sound the same but are written differently are called **enharmonic equivalents**.

One step further...

Building chords is easy—simply add intervals to the root. The type of intervals used determines the resulting chord type. Let's start by learning some basic three-note chords built on a C root:

Major chords contain a
M3 and a P5 on the root.

Minor chords contain a
m3 and a P5 on the root.

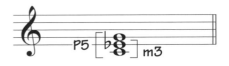

Once you're familiar with basic chord types, tons of other chords can be built simply by adding, subtracting, augmenting, or diminishing intervals.

BUILDING TO SCALE

The notes of a chord can also be determined by assigning a numeric **formula**, indicating the tones used from the major scale. For example, based on the C major scale, 1-♭3-5 would mean play the root (C), a flatted third (E♭), and the fifth (G)—a C minor chord!

The chart below is a construction summary of the chord types in this book (based on the key of C only):

C MAJOR SCALE = C-D-E-F-G-A-B-C

(1 2 3 4 5 6 7 1)

Chord type	Formula	Note names	Chord names
major	1-3-5	C-E-G	C
minor	1-♭3-5	C-E♭-G	Cm
augmented	1-3-♯5	C-E-G♯	C+
diminished	1-♭3-♭5	C-E♭-G♭	C°
suspended fourth	1-4-5	C-F-G	Csus4
suspended second	1-2-5	C-D-G	Csus2
added ninth	1-3-5-9	C-E-G-D	Cadd9
minor added ninth	1-♭3-5-9	C-E♭-G-D	Cm(add9)
fifth	1-5	C-G	C5
sixth	1-3-5-6	C-E-G-A	C6
minor sixth	1-♭3-5-6	C-E♭-G-A	Cm6
sixth, added ninth	1-3-5-6-9	C-E-G-A-D	C6/9
minor sixth, added ninth	1-♭3-5-6-9	C-E♭-G-A-D	Cm6/9
seventh	1-3-5-♭7	C-E-G-B♭	C7
diminished seventh	1-♭3-♭5-♭♭7	C-E♭-G♭-B♭♭	C°7
seventh, suspended fourth	1-4-5-♭7	C-F-G-B♭	C7sus4
major seventh	1-3-5-7	C-E-G-B	Cmaj7
minor seventh	1-♭3-5-♭7	C-E♭-G-B♭	Cm7
minor, major seventh	1-♭3-5-7	C-E♭-G-B	Cm(maj7)
major seventh, flat fifth	1-3-♭5-7	C-E-G♭-B	Cmaj7♭5
minor seventh, flat fifth	1-♭3-♭5-♭7	C-E♭-G♭-B♭	Cm7♭5
augmented seventh	1-3-♯5-♭7	C-E-G♯-B♭	C+7
seventh, flat fifth	1-3-♭5-♭7	C-E-G♭-B♭	C7♭5
seventh, flat ninth	1-3-5-♭7-♭9	C-E-G-B♭-D♭	C7♭9
seventh, sharp ninth	1-3-5-♭7-♯9	C-E-G-B♭-D♯	C7♯9
augmented seventh, flat ninth	1-3-♯5-♭7-♭9	C-E-G♯-B♭-D♭	C+7♭9
ninth	1-3-5-♭7-9	C-E-G-B♭-D	C9
major ninth	1-3-5-7-9	C-E-G-B-D	Cmaj9
minor ninth	1-♭3-5-♭7-9	C-E♭-G-B♭-D	Cm9
eleventh	1-3-5-♭7-9-11	C-E-G-B♭-D-F	C11
minor eleventh	1-♭3-5-♭7-9-11	C-E♭-G-B♭-D-F	Cm11
thirteenth	1-3-5-♭7-9-11-13	C-E-G-B♭-D-F-A	C13

☞ NOTE: Since the ukulele has only four strings, certain notes must sometimes be left out. And sometimes certain other notes are "doubled" (played twice). In general, the fifth and root are the first two pitches omitted when necessary.

CHOOSING THE BEST VOICING

Each chord can have several different **voicings.** A voicing is the same chord but with a rearrangement of the notes (which means you'll also have to rearrange your hand and finger positions). For each individual chord, this book gives you **four** voicings to choose from... you're welcome!

Decisions, decisions...

Although (in theory) you may use any of the four voicings in any situation, each group does suggest a specialized function. A chord's location, difficulty, size, and intended musical style all contribute to this determination. Here's how each of the four voicings were chosen and how they should be used:

Voicing #1

The top diagram is the most common voicing in **open position** (or as nearby as possible). It's appropriate for strumming and usually fingerpicking as well.

Voicing #2

This diagram is usually another voicing that's moved slightly up the neck. It's a good all-purpose voicing as well. In some cases, however, this will be an alternative to Voicing 1 if an open string can be creatively incorporated.

Voicing #3

Even farther up the neck, this voicing (as with Voicing 2) is especially useful for playing solo arrangements, when you may need to play melody notes in higher registers.

Voicing #4

This voicing will change depending on the chord type.

- For triads (such as major and minor chords), it will be a three-string, **moveable** (i.e., it contains no open strings) voicing that may or may not contain a muted string. In other words, it could be built off adjacent string groups, such as 4-3-2 or 3-2-1, or it may use nonadjacent string groups, such as 4-2-1 or 4-3-1. For the nonadjacent string-group voicings, you'll need to mute the unused string with one of your fretting fingers in order to strum the voicing.
- For chords containing more than three different notes (such as seventh chords or add chords), this will be another up-the-neck voicing option.

Keep in mind that different moveable voicings will be used for different root notes. In other words, you may find different moveable voicings for A9 than you do for G9. Therefore, we encourage you to look through all the keys for each chord type if you want to explore as many different voicings as possible.

Note: As it is common practice in many styles to omit the third from a dominant eleventh chord, voicings with and without the third are included for this chord type.

Alright already!

Don't get too bogged down with all this "theory" stuff. Just look up the chords you need and learn to play them. Heck, make up your own chords—if it sounds good, play it! If you come across a chord type not listed in this book (and you will eventually), either build the chord with the intervals named in the suffix or reduce it to a more common seventh or ninth chord.

Just in case...

Here's how to read the fingerboard diagrams in this book:

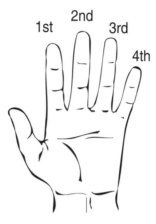

Think of your fretting-hand fingers as being numbered 1 through 4.

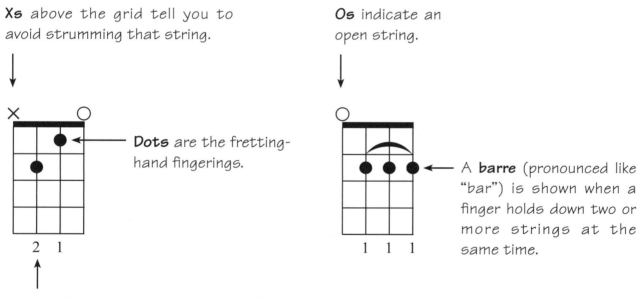

Xs above the grid tell you to avoid strumming that string.

Dots are the fretting-hand fingerings.

Numbers below the strings tell you which finger to use on that string.

Os indicate an open string.

A **barre** (pronounced like "bar") is shown when a finger holds down two or more strings at the same time.

NOTE: **Fret numbers** ("5fr") may appear to the right of the first fret on some chord diagrams. This tells you to slide your hand up to the appropriate fret, position your fingers, and strum away. If no fret number is shown (or you see a thick top line on the diagram), your hand should be around fret 1, near the **nut**.

CHORDS

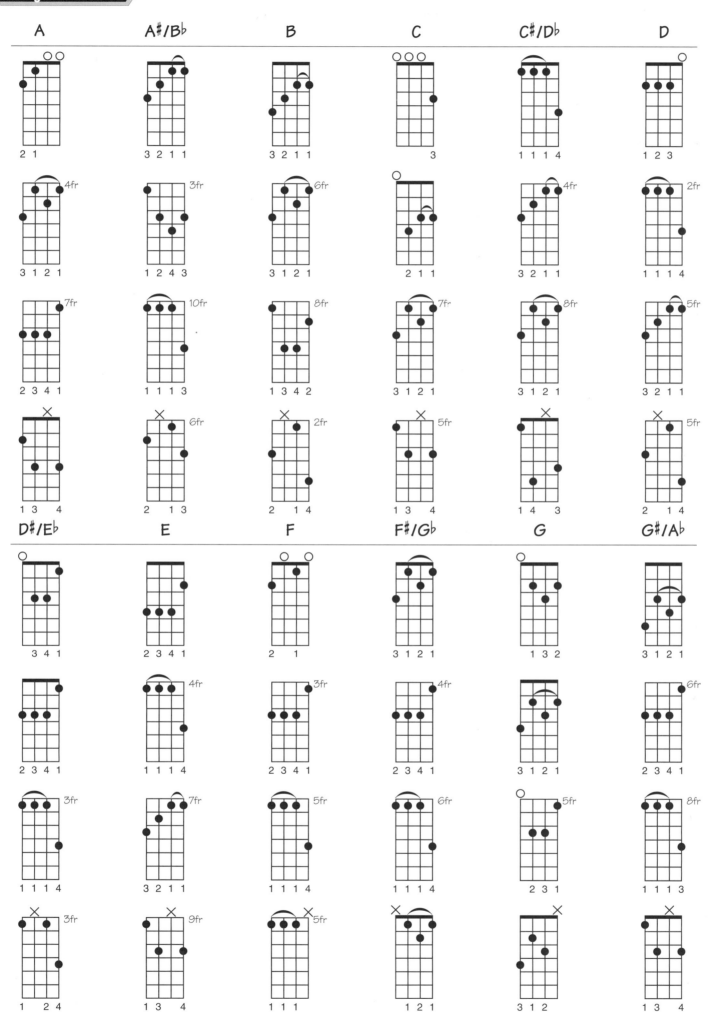

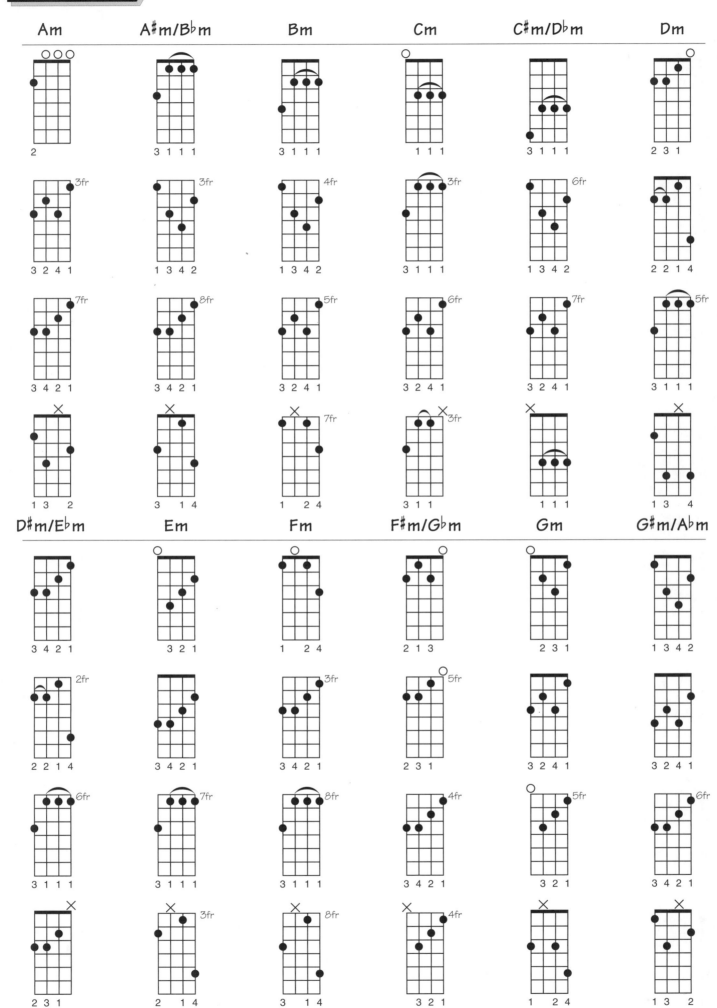

Augmented

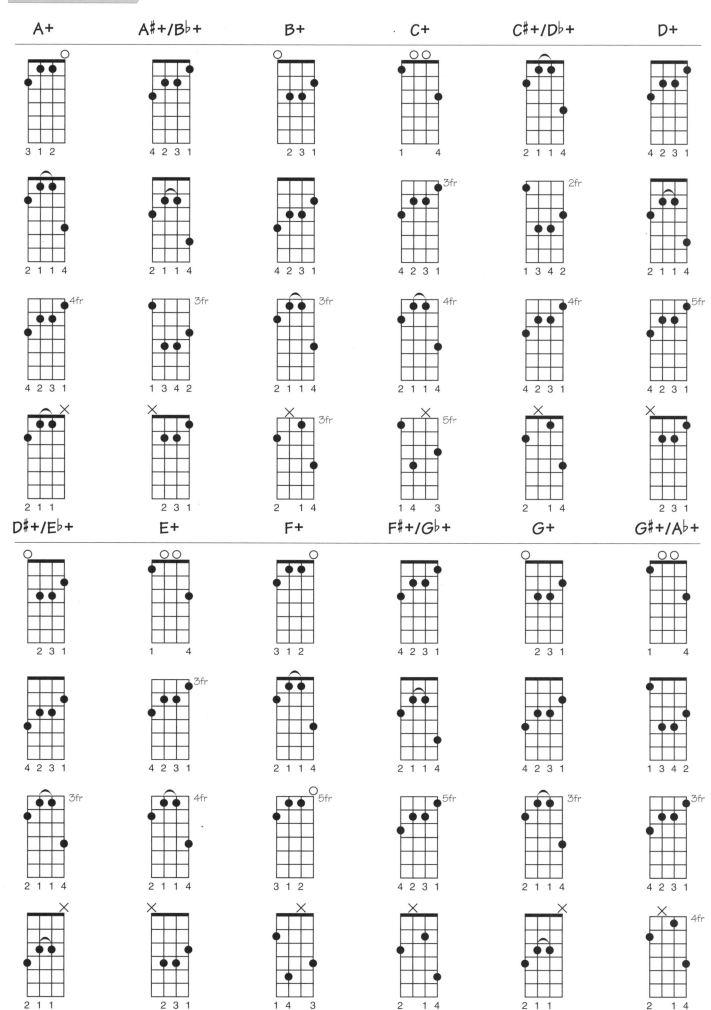

Diminished

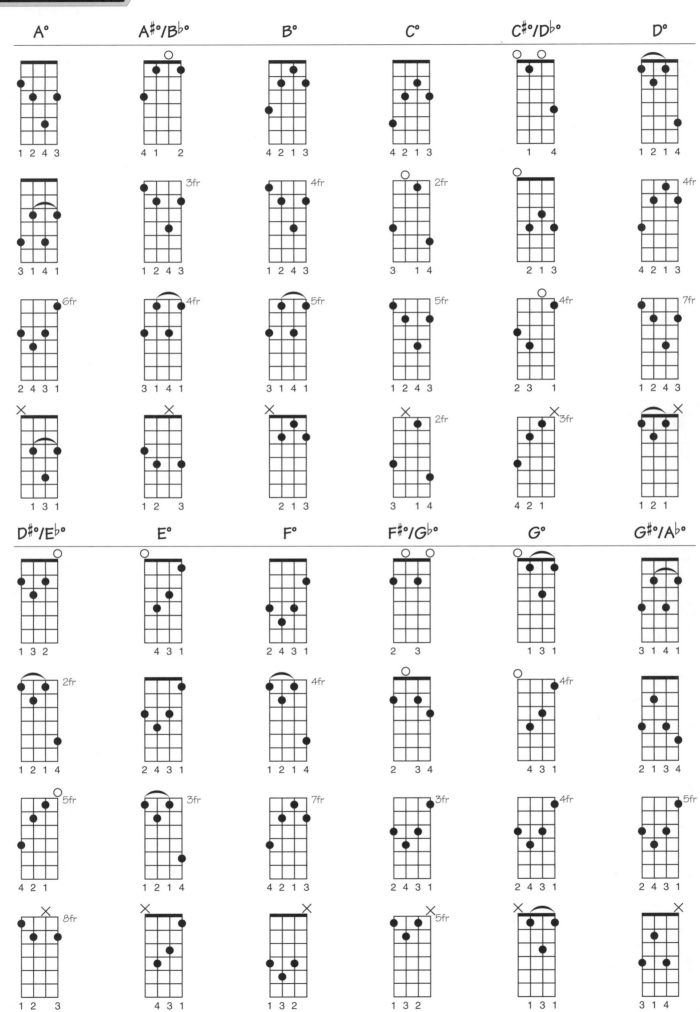

Suspended Fourth

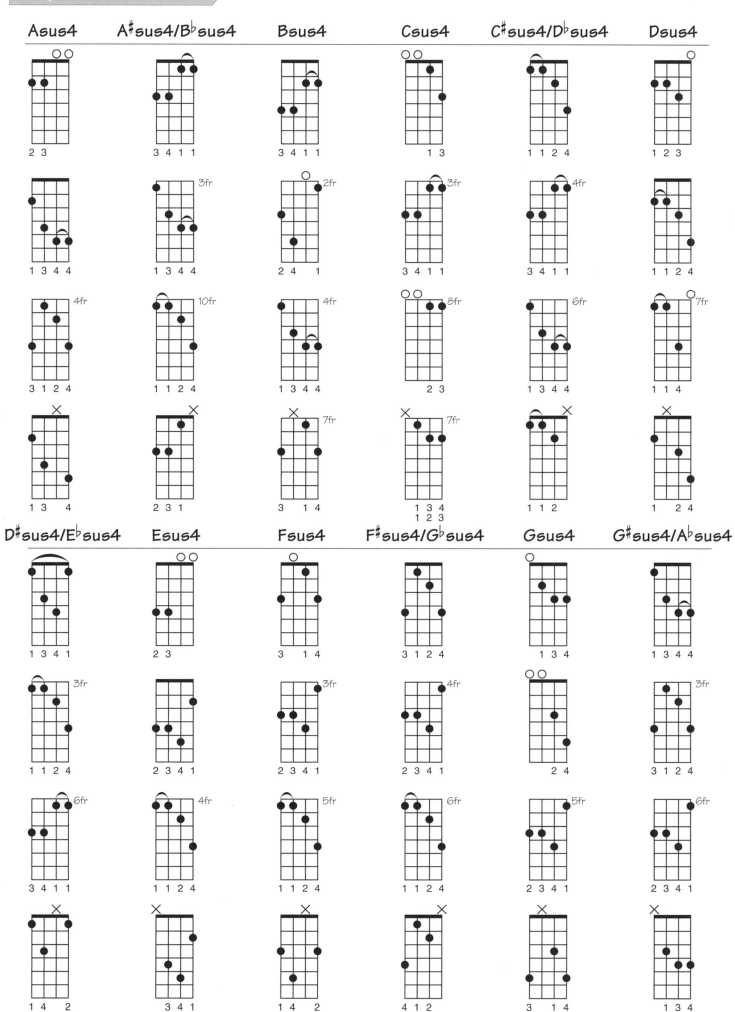

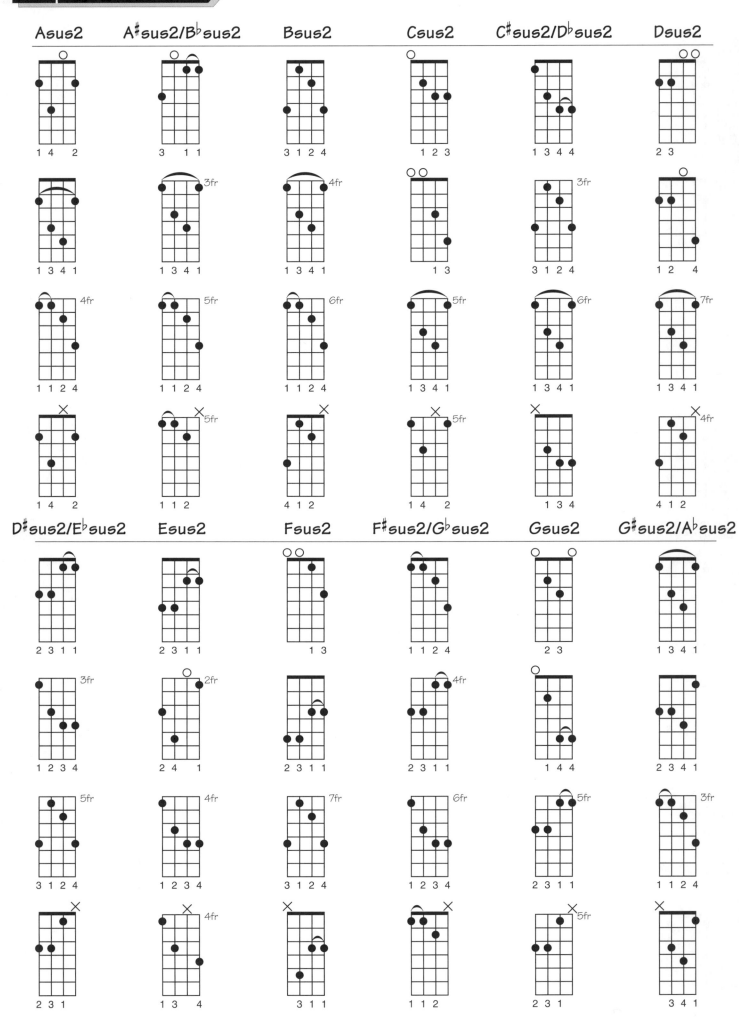

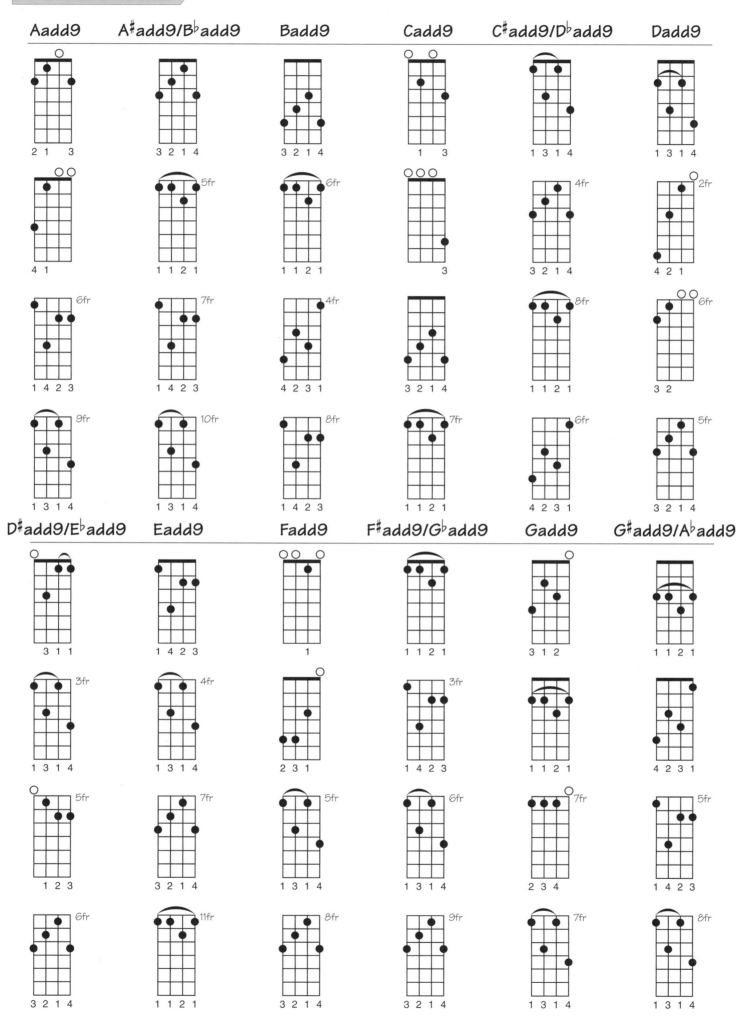

Minor Added Ninth

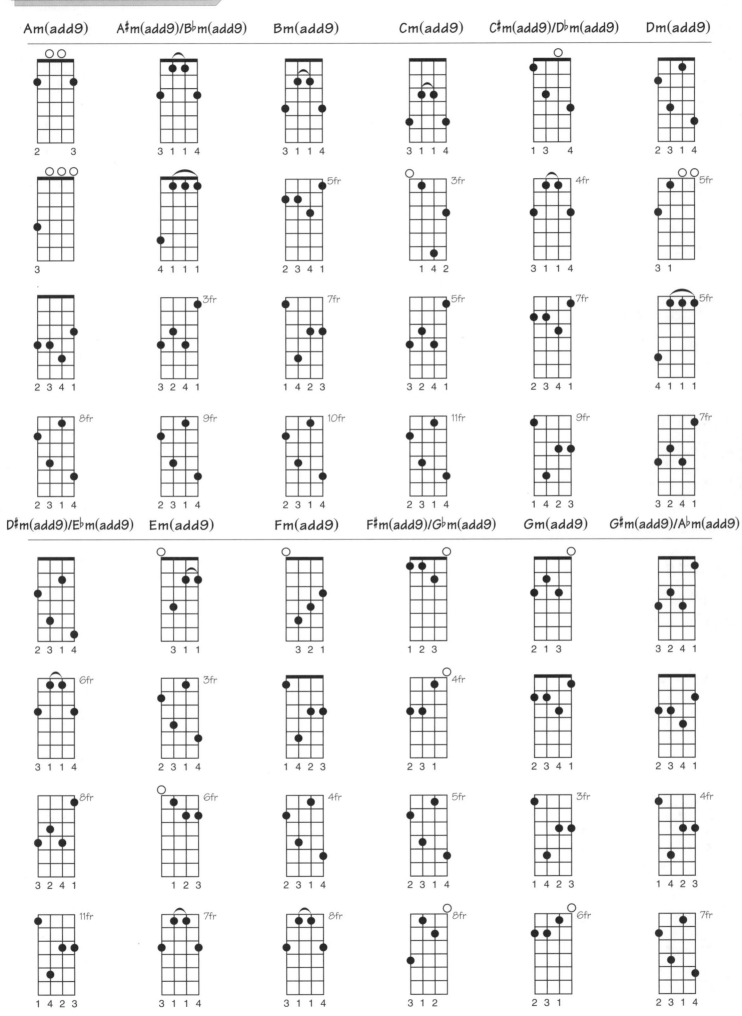

Am(add9)   A#m(add9)/B♭m(add9)   Bm(add9)   Cm(add9)   C#m(add9)/D♭m(add9)   Dm(add9)

D#m(add9)/E♭m(add9)   Em(add9)   Fm(add9)   F#m(add9)/G♭m(add9)   Gm(add9)   G#m(add9)/A♭m(add9)

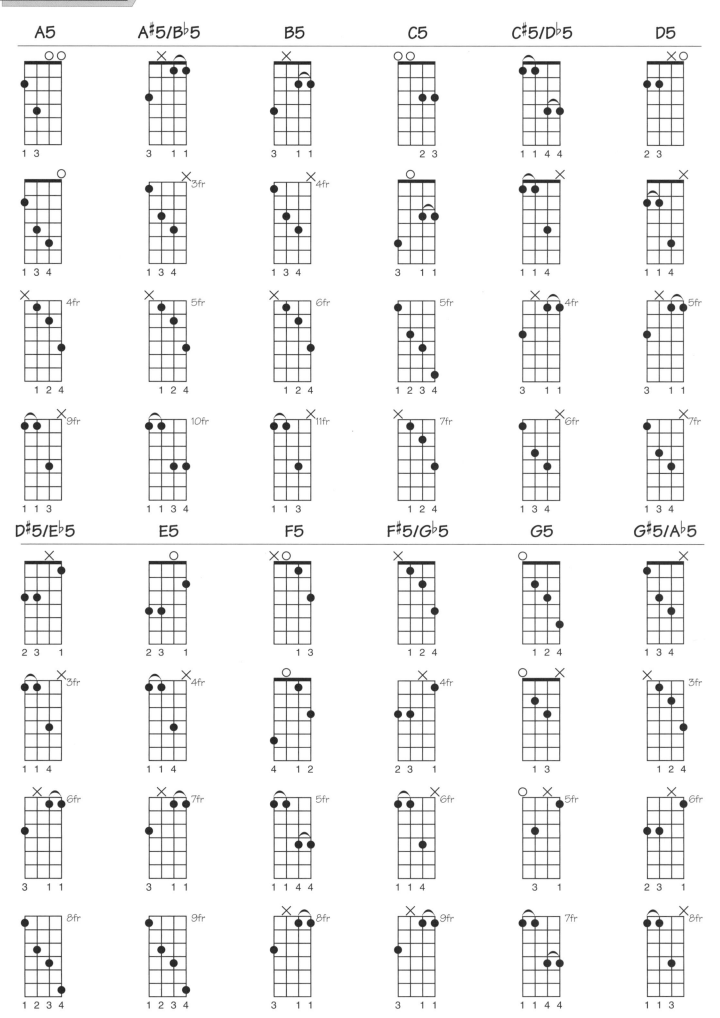

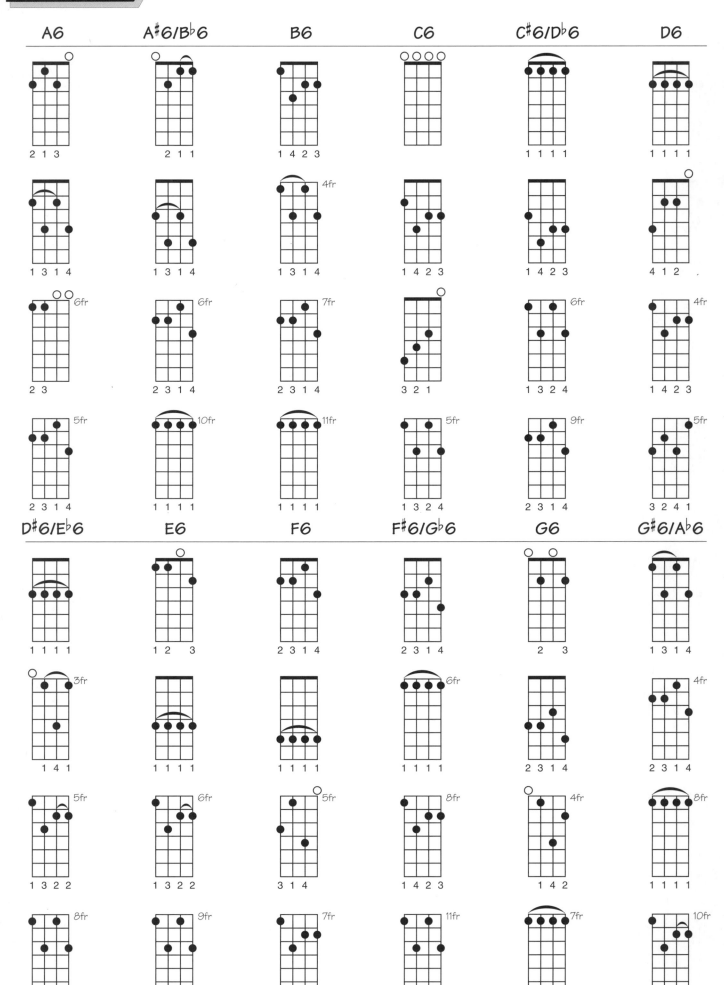

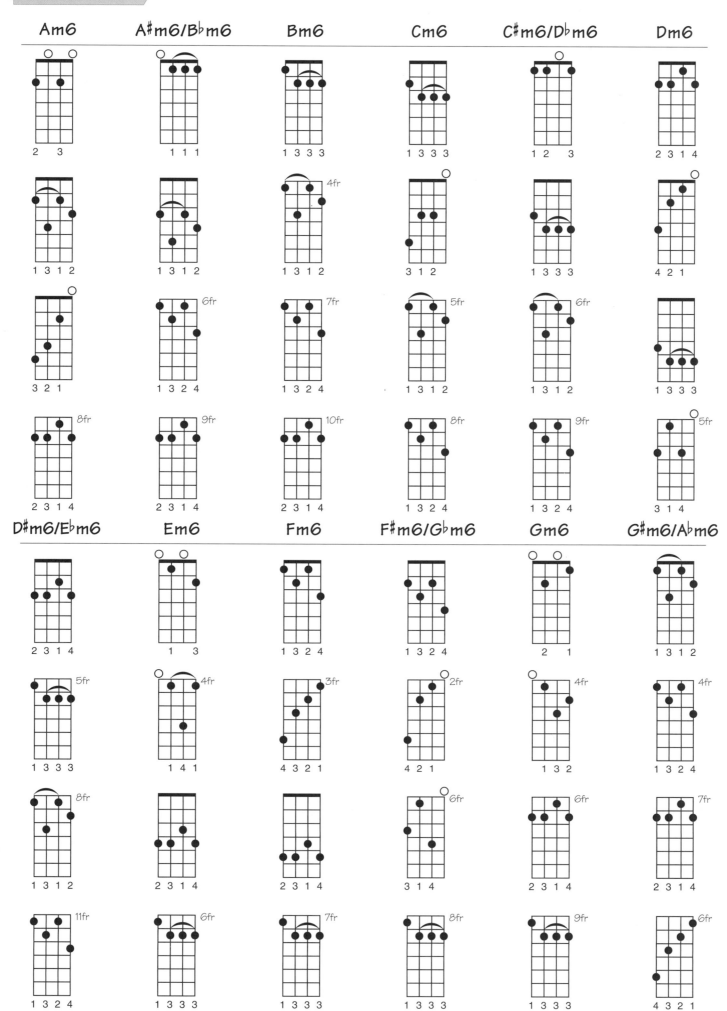

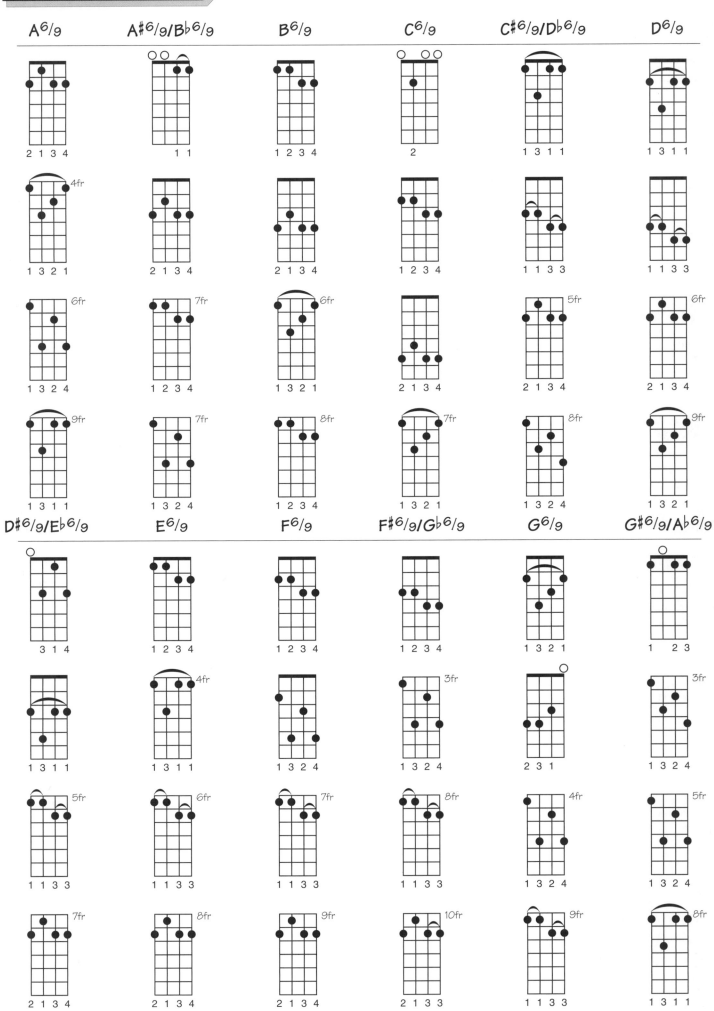

Minor Sixth, Added Ninth

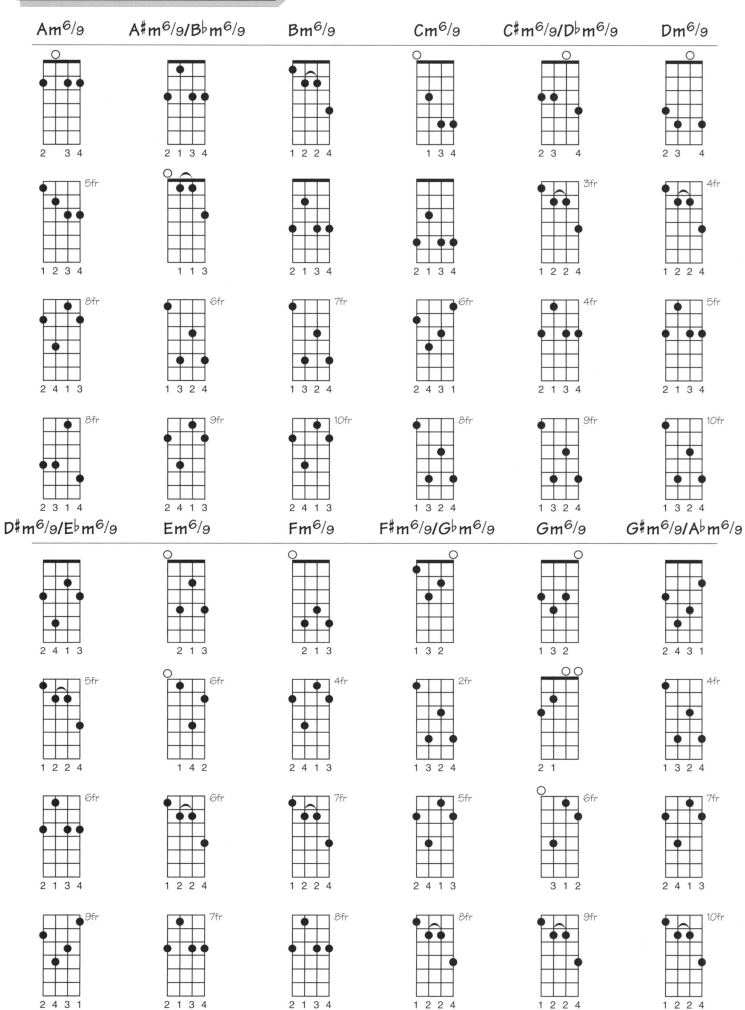

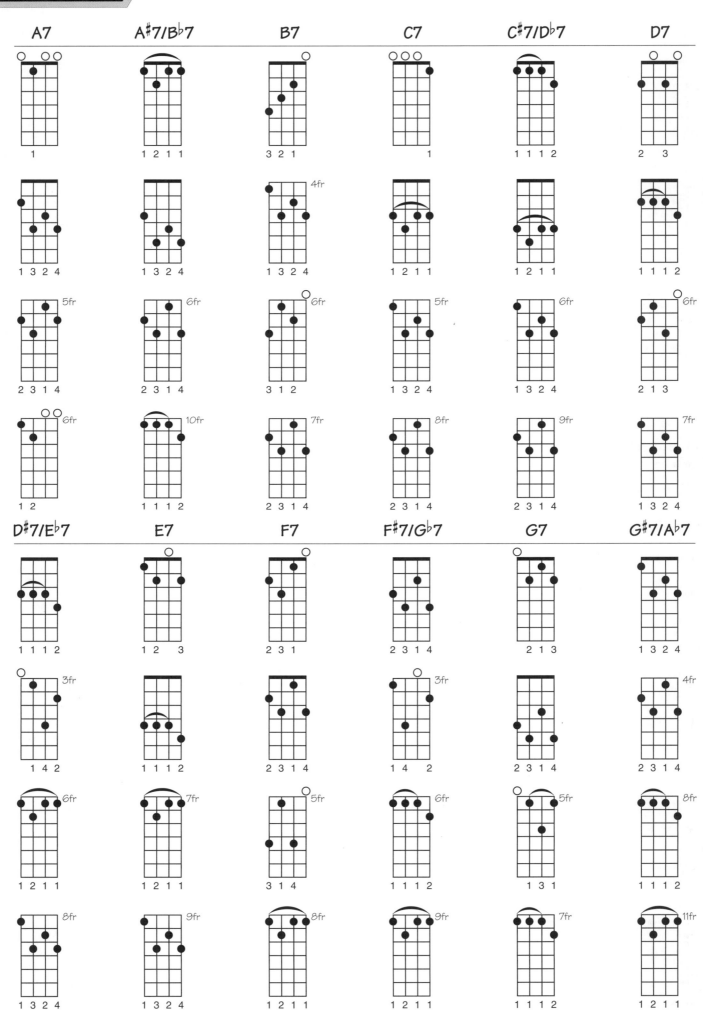

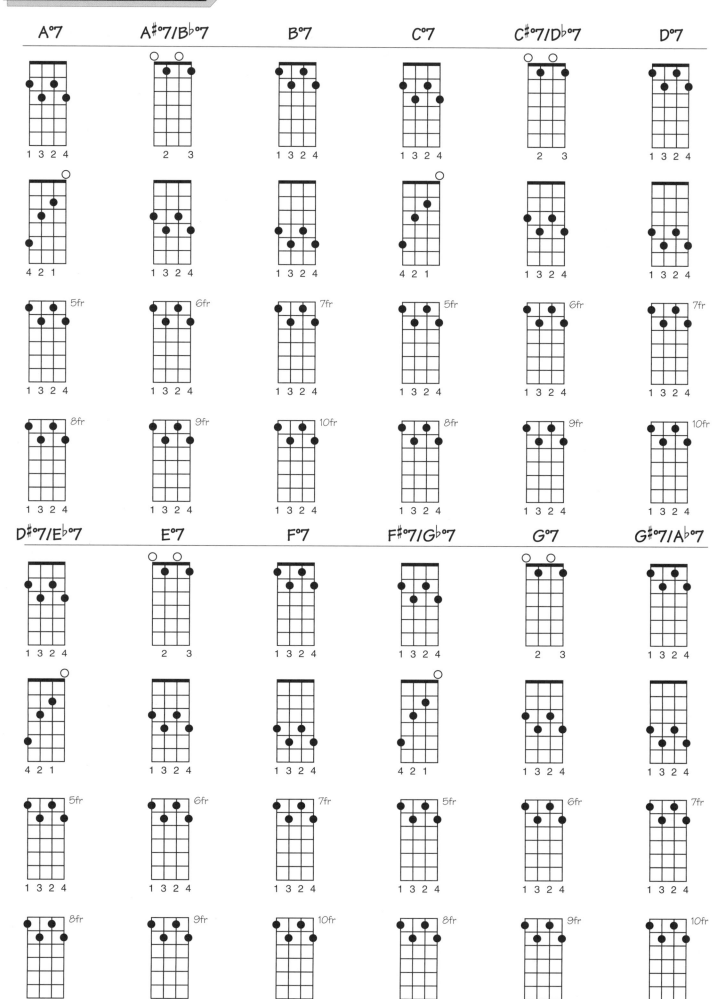

Seventh, Suspended Fourth

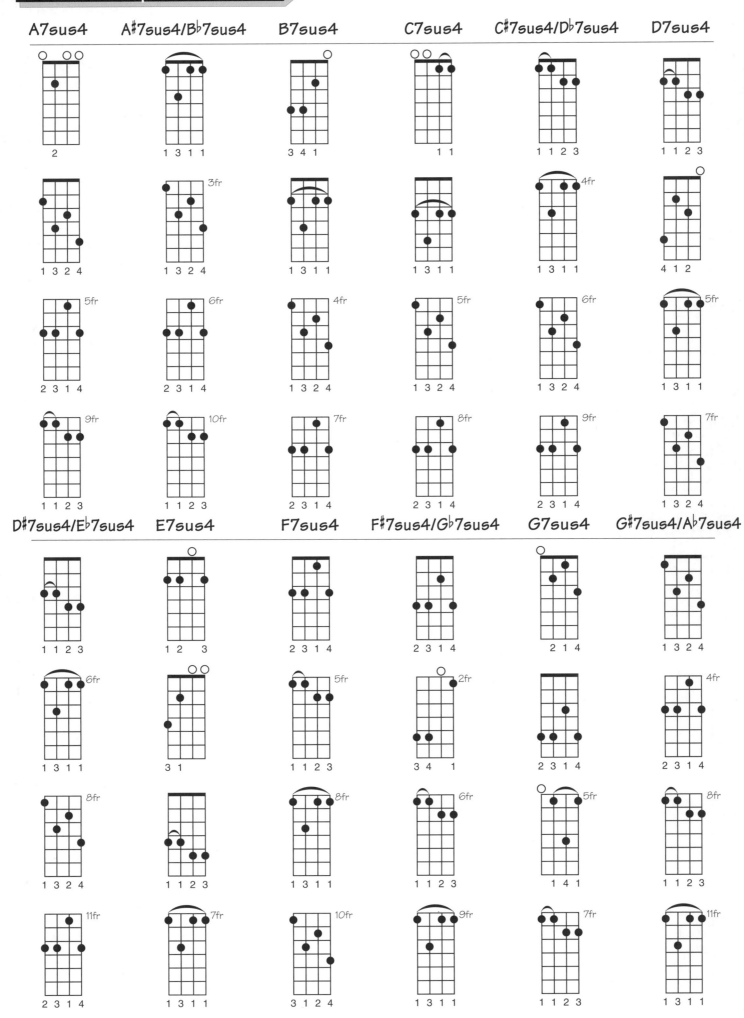

A7sus4   A#7sus4/B♭7sus4   B7sus4   C7sus4   C#7sus4/D♭7sus4   D7sus4

D#7sus4/E♭7sus4   E7sus4   F7sus4   F#7sus4/G♭7sus4   G7sus4   G#7sus4/A♭7sus4

Major Seventh

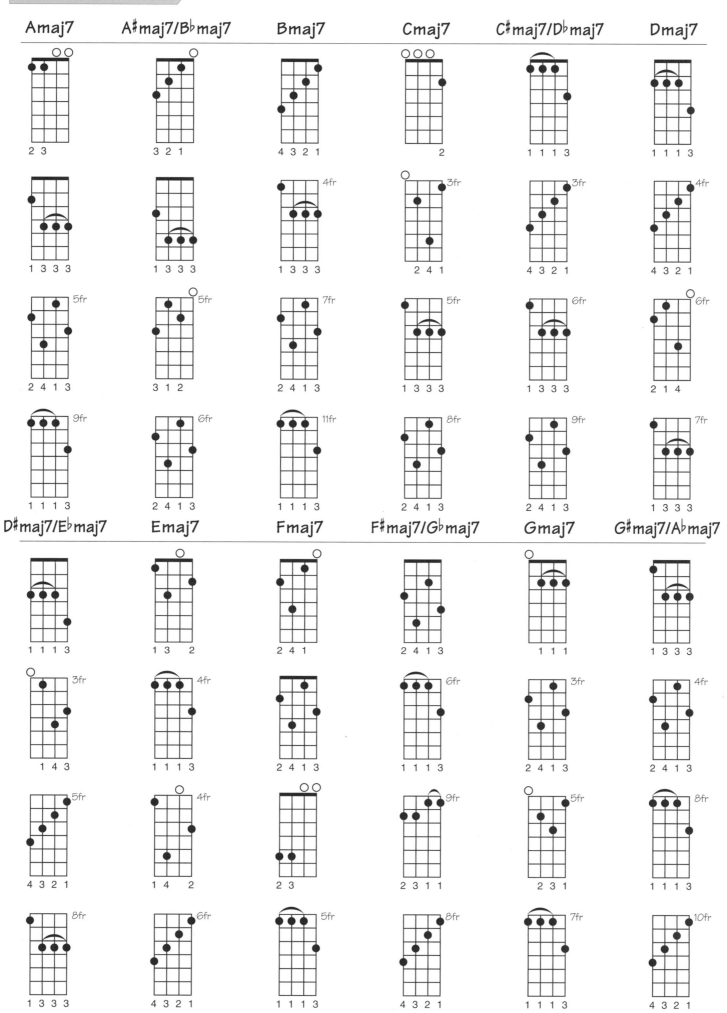

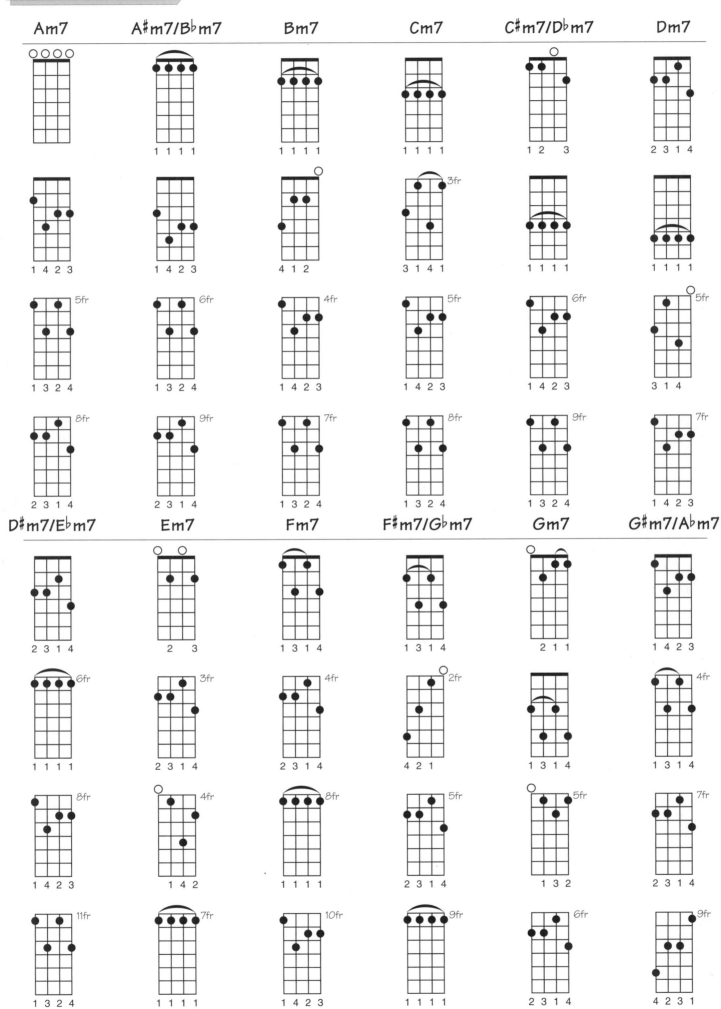

Minor, Major Seventh

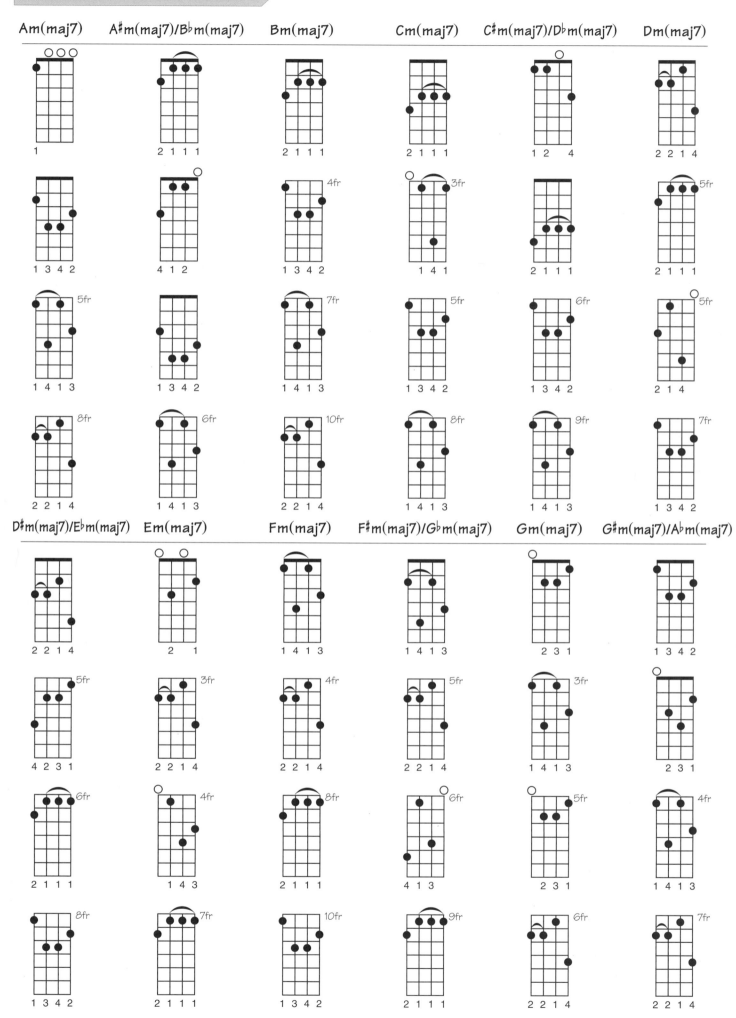

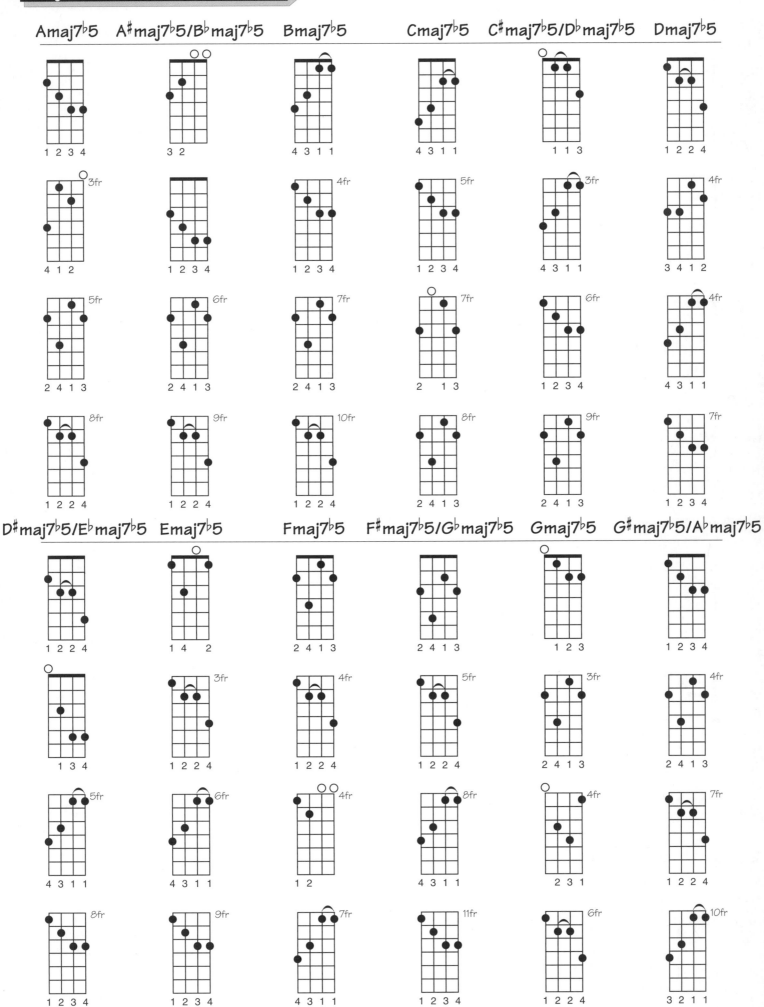

Minor Seventh, Flat Fifth

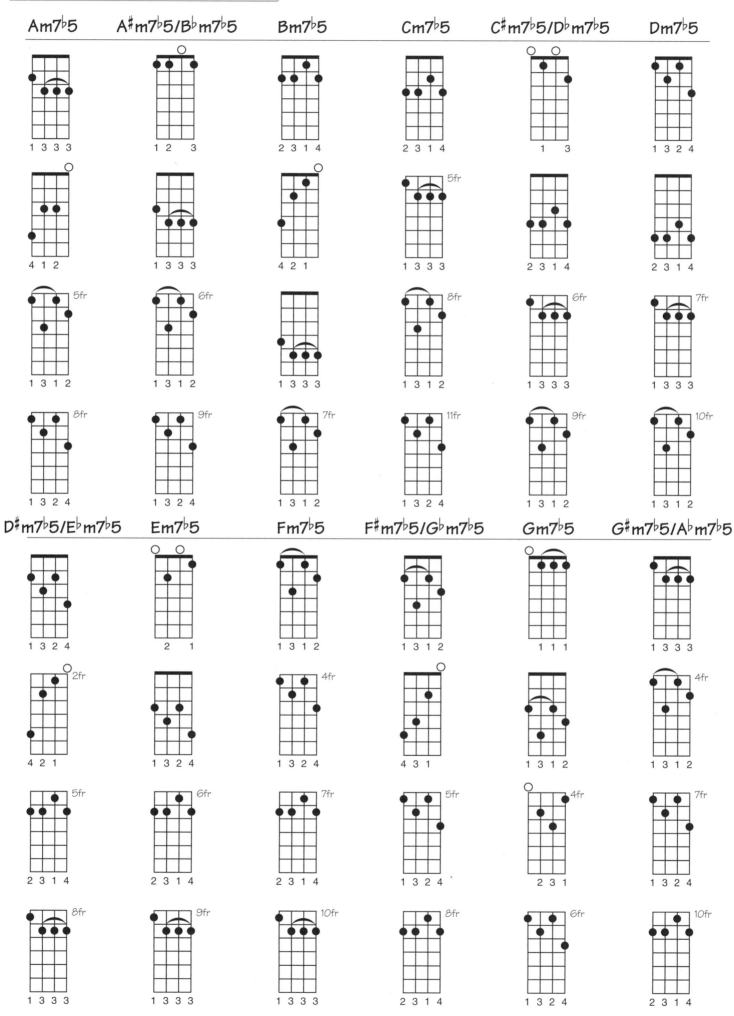

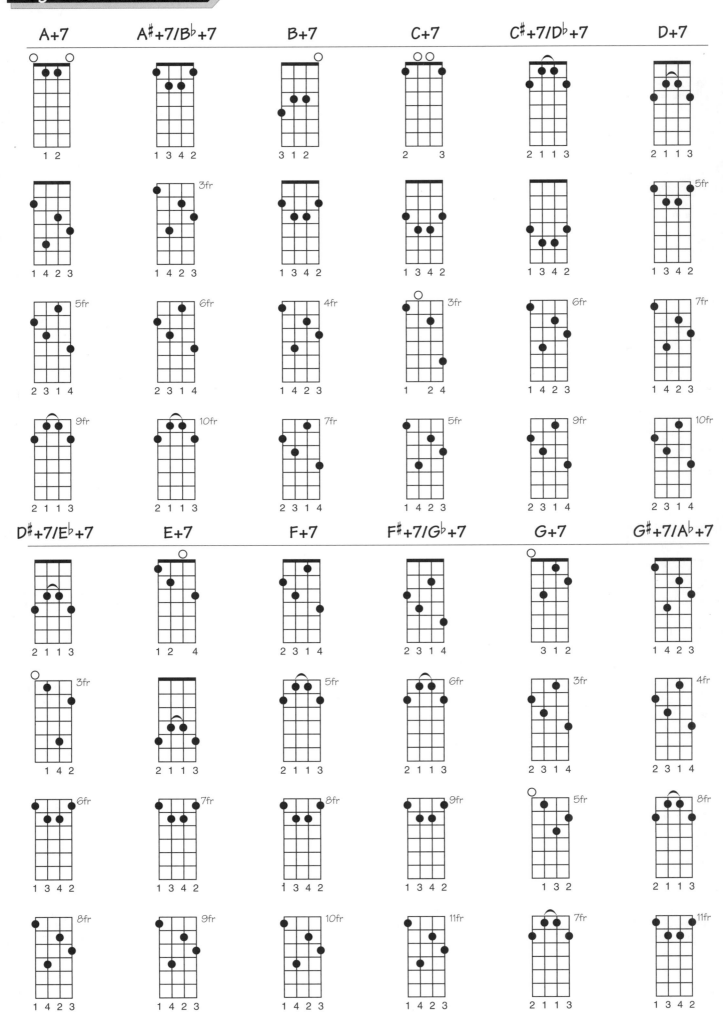

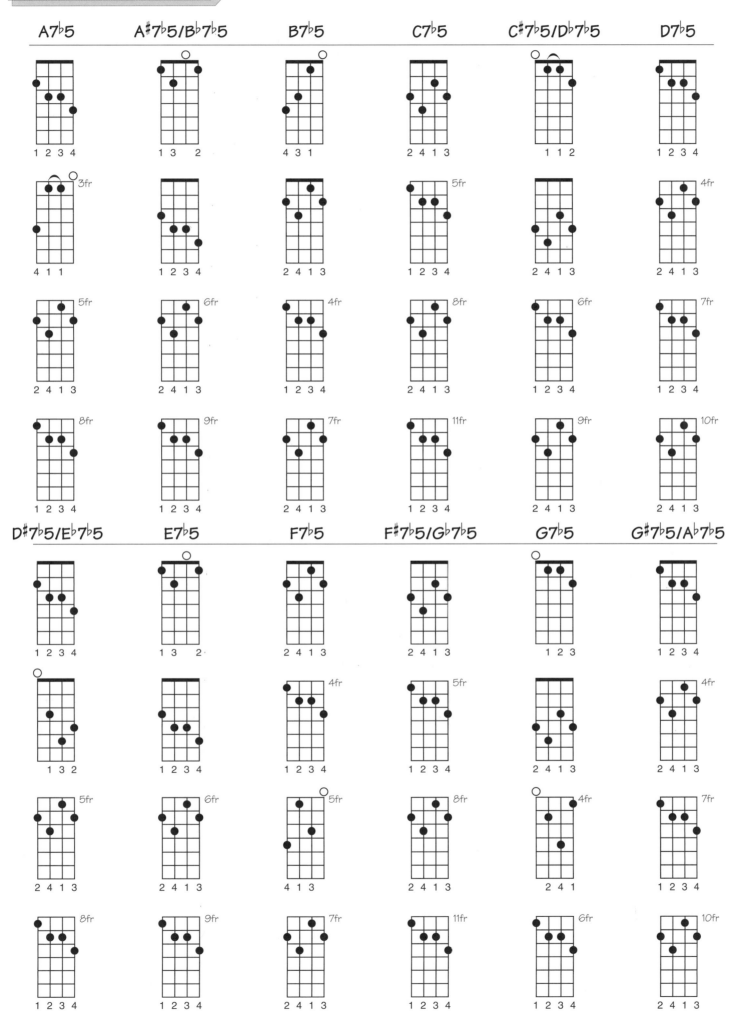

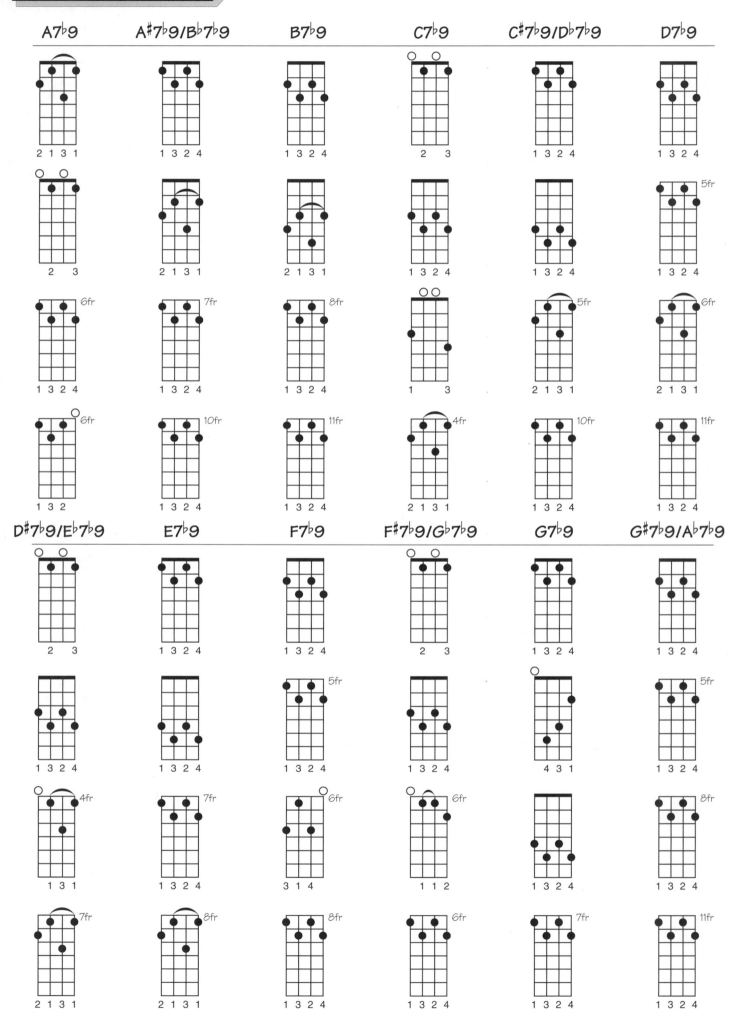

Seventh, Sharp Ninth

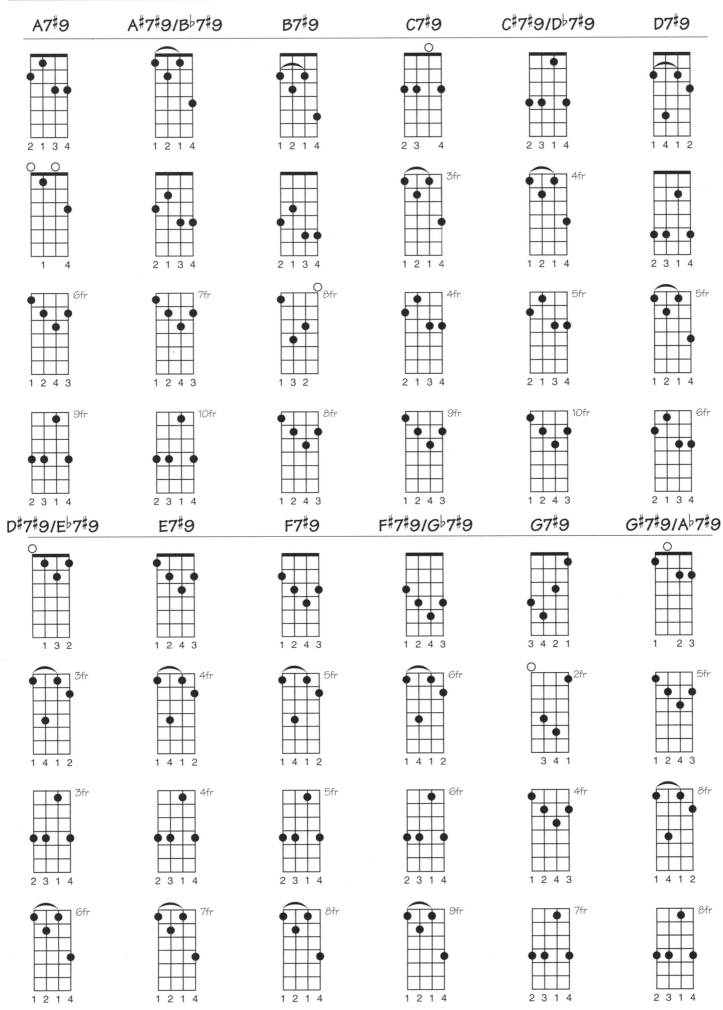

35

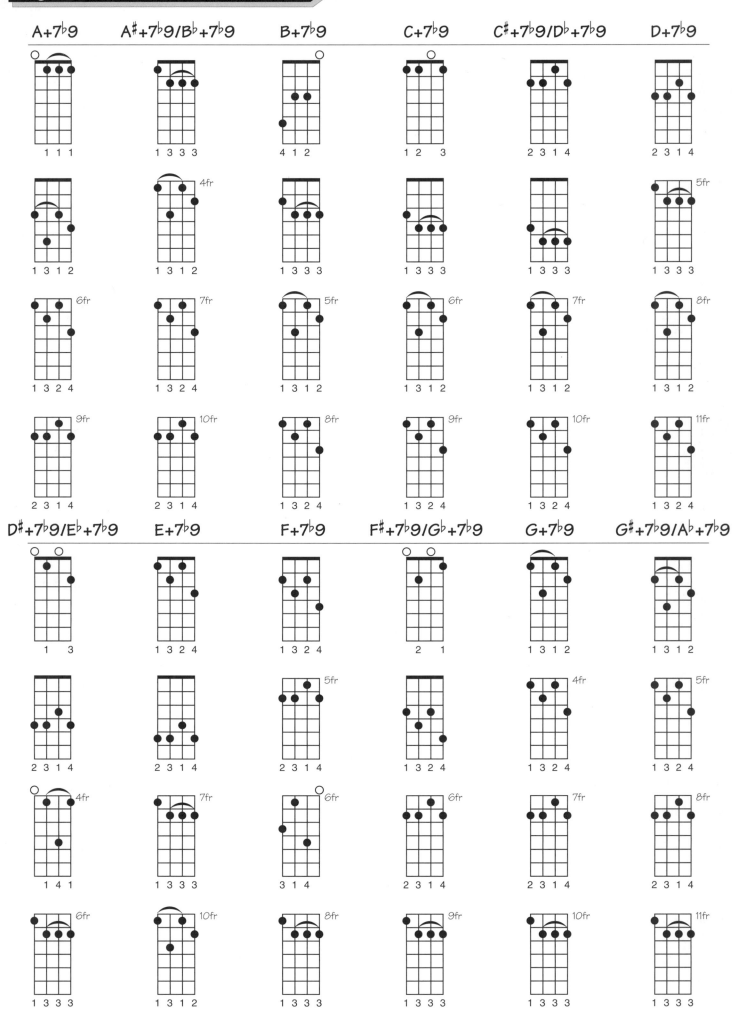

A+7♭9 A♯+7♭9/B♭+7♭9 B+7♭9 C+7♭9 C♯+7♭9/D♭+7♭9 D+7♭9

D♯+7♭9/E♭+7♭9 E+7♭9 F+7♭9 F♯+7♭9/G♭+7♭9 G+7♭9 G♯+7♭9/A♭+7♭9

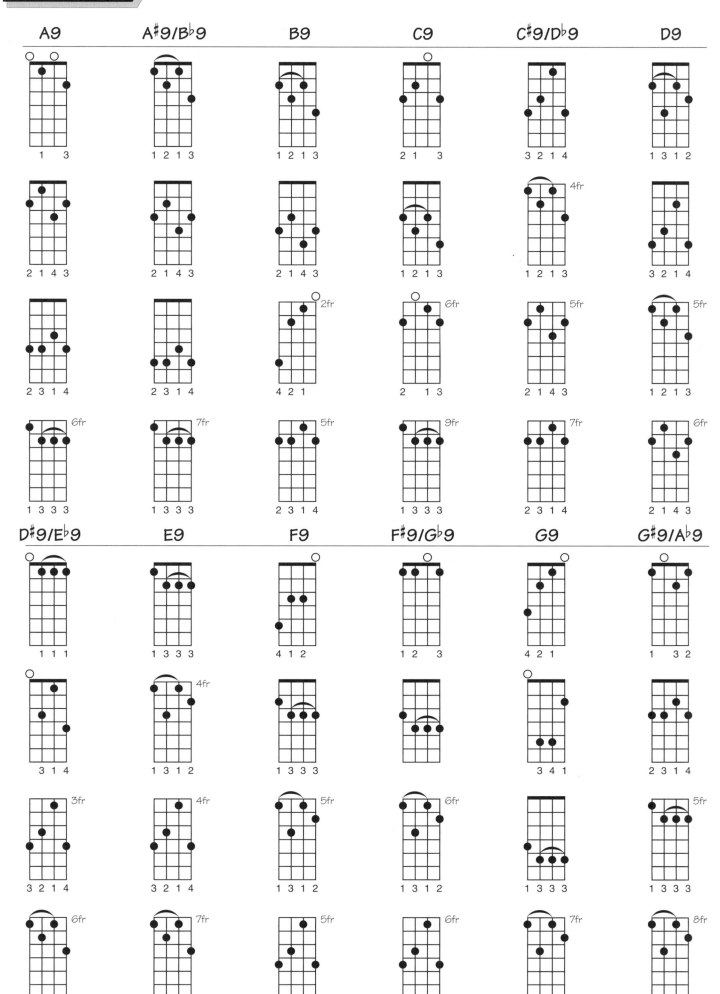

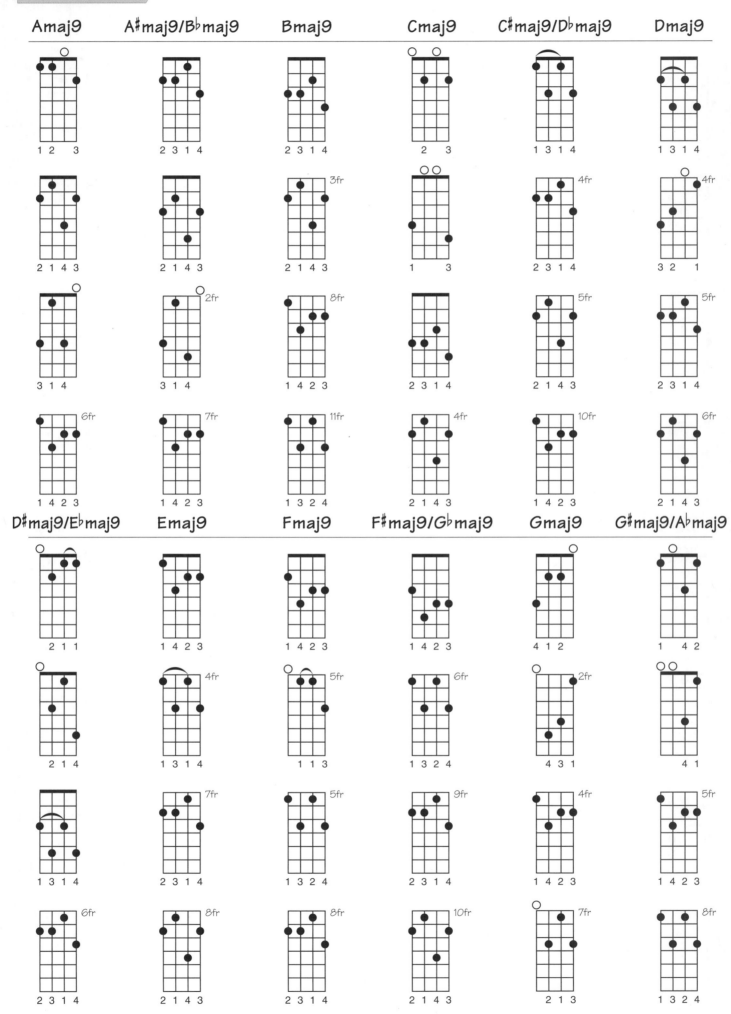

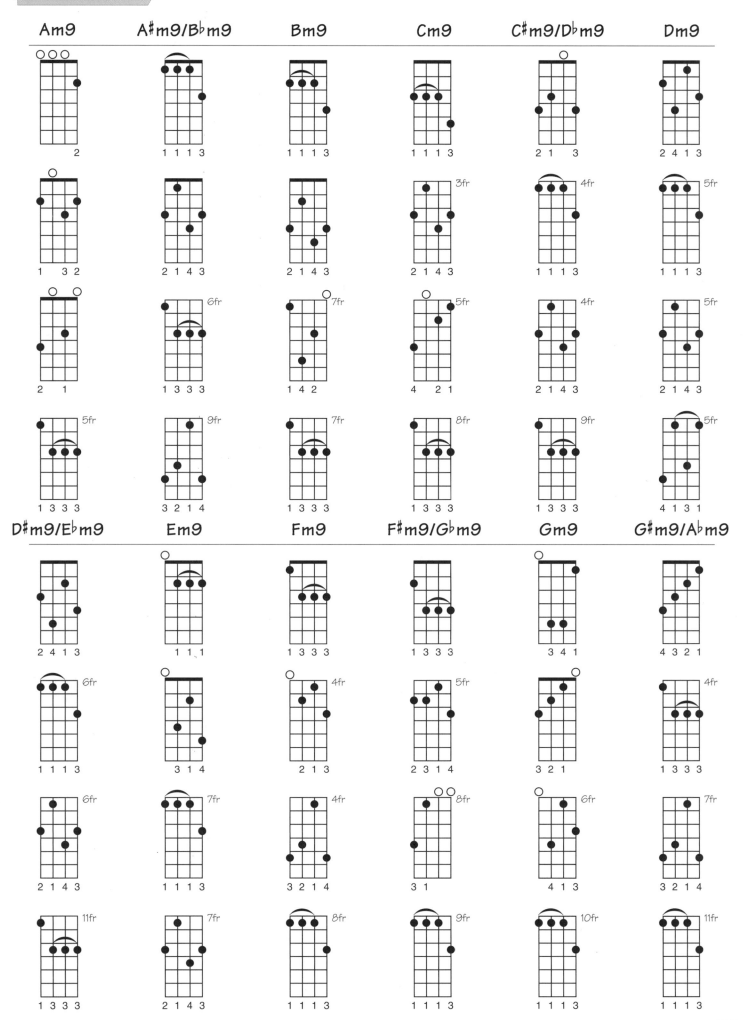

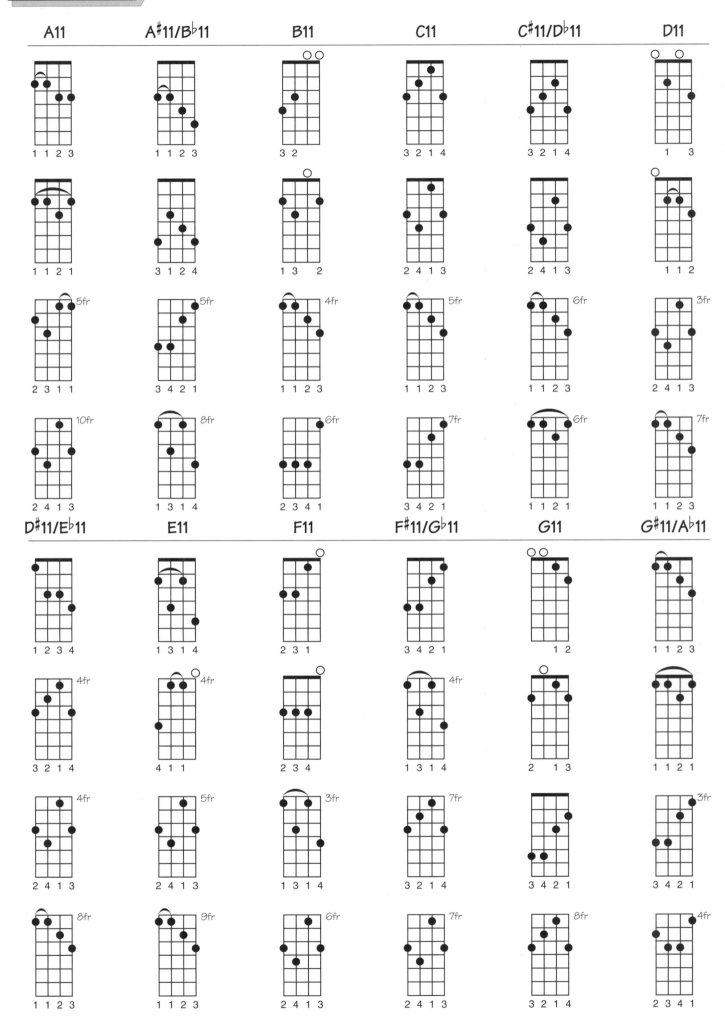

Minor Eleventh

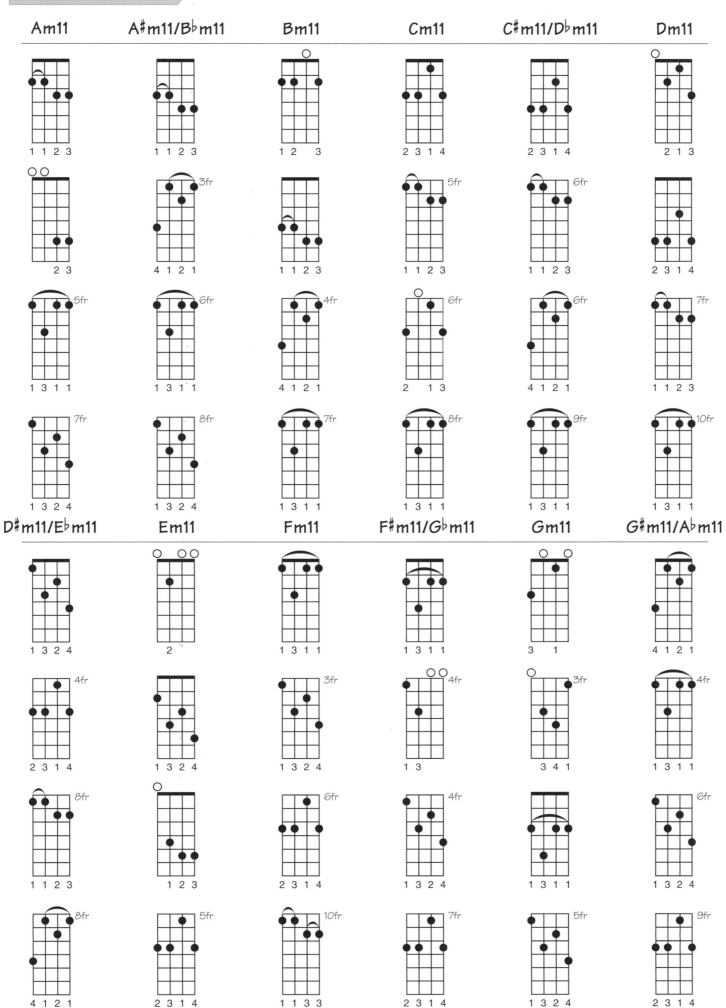

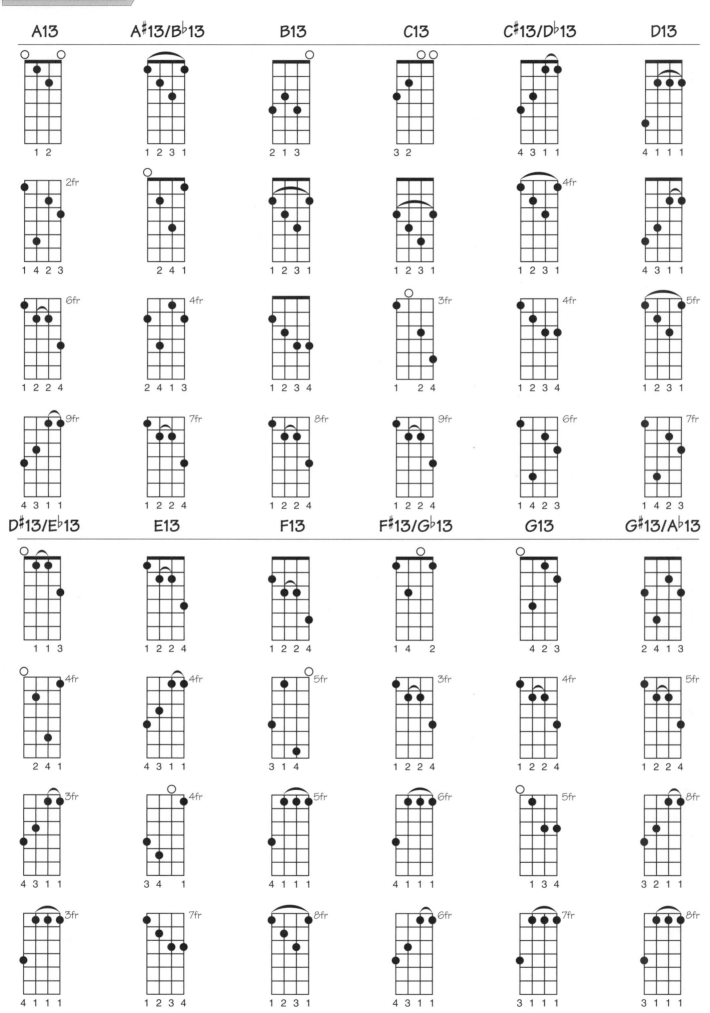

SCALES

SCALES

Scale (from L. *scala*, ladder): A progression of notes in a specific order.

Scales are very important to know, especially when it comes to playing a solo. This section is an easy reference for constructing, locating, and playing all the essential scales on your ukulele. By the end of this section, you'll be using scales to improvise over the "Jam Session" audio tracks.

Essential ingredients...

We've given you three ways to build (or "spell") each scale:

1. Step Pattern *(ex. W–H–W–W–H–W+H–H)*

This pattern tells you how many steps to move from one scale tone to the next, using abbreviations for whole step (W), half step (H), and 1 1/2 steps (W+H). Simply start on any note and move up accordingly.

Here's an example starting on the root note A:

step pattern	=	W–W–H–W–W–W–H
result	=	A–B–C#–D–E–F#–G#–A

2. Formula *(ex. 1–2–♭3–4–5–♭6–7–1)*

Take the numbers in the formula (which correspond to a particular major scale tone) and alter them as indicated by the flats and/or sharps. Try this one...

A major scale	=	A–B–C#–D–E–F#–G#–A
formula	=	1–2–♭3–4–5–♭6–7–1
result	=	A–B–C–D–E–F–G–A

IMPORTANT: These formulas are always based on the **major scale** (including any sharps or flats) not just the letter names of the notes. That is, 3 for the key of E major is actually G# (not G). So, if the formula calls for ♭3, play G (one half step lower than G#) not G♭.

3. Note Name *(ex. A–B–C–D–E–F–G–A)*

Although we don't have room to show all the scales on all twelve root notes (actually seventeen if you count the enharmonics!), the note names shown are relative to the root note used. Of course, a scale built on a different root note will have a different list of note names.

Let's get organized...

Several fretboard locations are given for each scale in this book. Use the one that feels the most comfortable for you. (Or, heck, memorize all of them!)

Form 1: From the Root

The fingerings in this system begin with the root note on string 3 and continue up an octave to the root note on string 1. This is a good "home base" fingering because it's framed nicely on the fingerboard and features the root as the lowest note.

Form 2: From the Third

This fingering begins with the scale's third degree on string 3 and continues up an octave to the scale's third on string 1. This is a great "in-between" form that nicely bridges Form 1 and Form 3.

Form 3: From the Fifth

This fingering begins with the scale's fifth degree on string 3 and continues up an octave to the fifth on string 1. This is another well-framed form and works nicely when you need to have access to notes above and below the root.

Form 4: Horizontal Form

These fingerings feature four notes on each string (three for the pentatonic scales) and span a full octave and a fifth, covering 11 frets or more. They'll require you to either slide or shift positions once per string when ascending or descending, but they're great for visualizing a big chunk of the fingerboard at once.

Get in sync!

Practicing scales requires both hands to work together in perfect synchronization. Strike each note clearly and precisely, making sure you pluck (or pick) and finger the note at exactly the same time. Remember to always alternate plucking fingers (or use **alternate picking**—successive downstrokes and upstrokes—if playing with a pick) to avoid excessive hand strain.

☞ **PRACTICE TIP:** Make sure you play each scale forward and then backward. And, as always, start out slowly and gradually increase the speed as you build up confidence.

MOVEABLE PATTERNS

All of the scale patterns given in this book are **moveable**—that is, they can be easily shifted up or down the fingerboard to accommodate any key or root note. To do this, take notice of the darkened root notes:

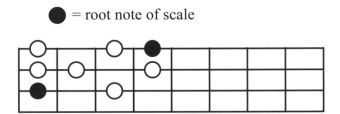

● = root note of scale

You can use any of these root notes as a point of reference for moving patterns. Since we'll be using only strings 3–1 on the ukulele for these diagrams (because of reentrant tuning), the roots located on strings 3 and 2 will likely be the most helpful.

root on third string   root on second string

To play the scale pattern in any particular key, match one of the root notes to its respective note on the fingerboard. (For example, the key of C has a root note of C.) The rest of the pattern follows accordingly—it's as simple as shifting the shape.

Check out the example below:

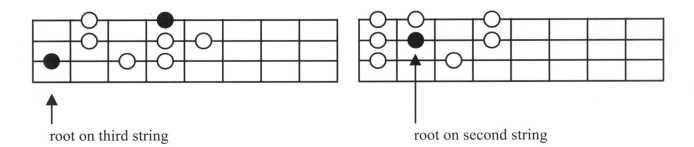

Moveable Major Scale Pattern	Beginning Fret (fret the root is on)	Resulting Scale
	fret 1	C#/Db major scale
	fret 3	Eb major scale
	fret 6	F#/Gb major scale
	fret 10	A#/Bb major scale
	fret 12	C major scale

Picture this...

Use the **Ukulele Fingerboard Chart** below to help you quickly locate all the notes within the first twelve frets. As described on the previous page, this chart will be especially useful as you begin using the moveable scale patterns in the pages ahead.

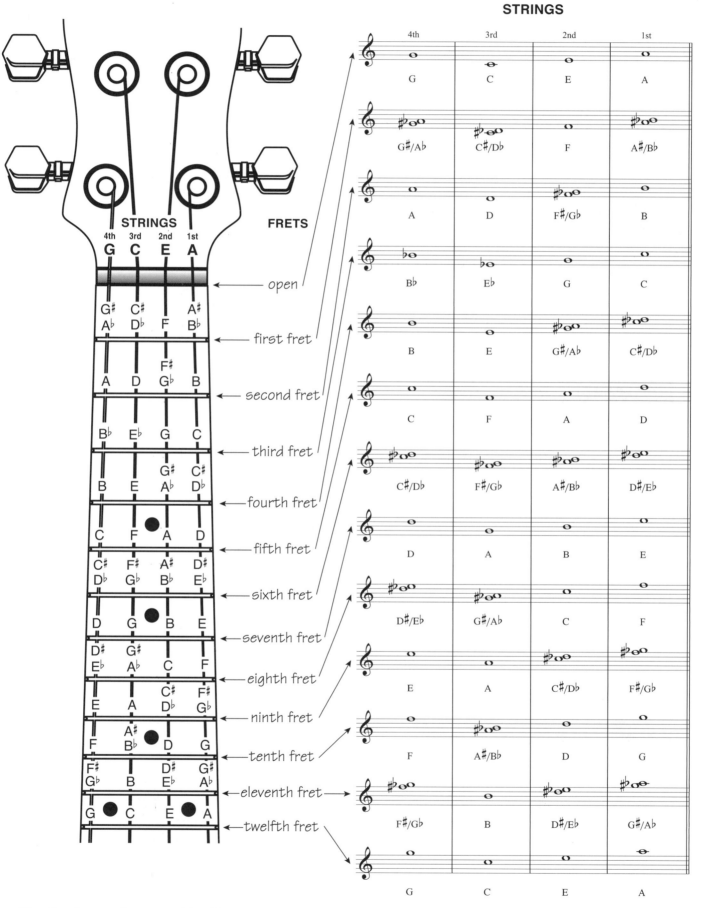

That's about all... good luck!

MAJOR

The most common scale used in music is the major scale, so learn it well! Like most scales, it consists of seven different notes.

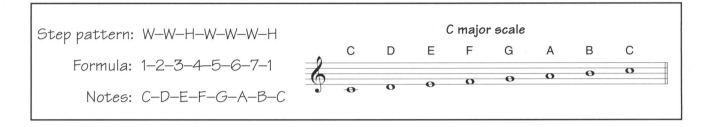

Step pattern: W–W–H–W–W–W–H

Formula: 1–2–3–4–5–6–7–1

Notes: C–D–E–F–G–A–B–C

C major scale

C D E F G A B C

Form 1: From the Root

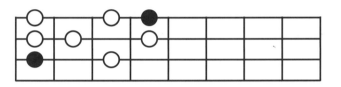

Form 2: From the Third

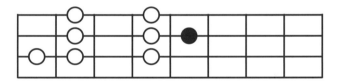

Form 3: From the Fifth

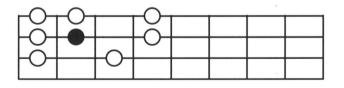

Form 4: Horizontal Form

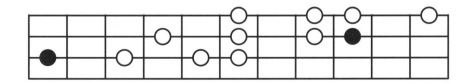

MINOR

This scale is used in nearly all styles of Western music. It's sometimes referred to as the "pure minor," "natural minor," "relative minor," or "Aeolian mode."

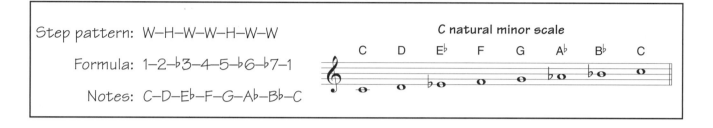

Step pattern: W–H–W–W–H–W–W

Formula: 1–2–♭3–4–5–♭6–♭7–1

Notes: C–D–E♭–F–G–A♭–B♭–C

Form 1: From the Root

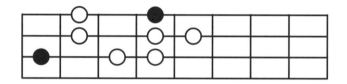

Form 2: From the Third

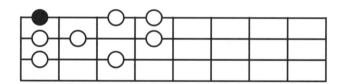

Form 3: From the Fifth

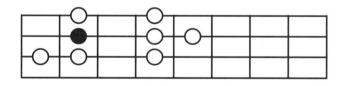

Form 4: Horizontal Form

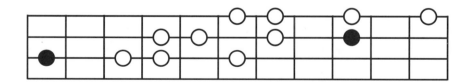

HARMONIC MINOR

This scale provides another alternative minor scale type and is very common in classical music.

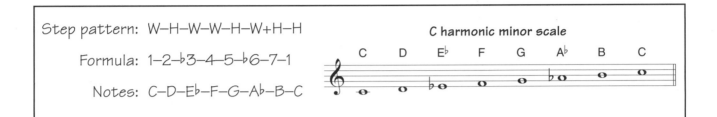

Step pattern: W–H–W–W–H–W+H–H

Formula: 1–2–♭3–4–5–♭6–7–1

Notes: C–D–E♭–F–G–A♭–B–C

C harmonic minor scale

Form 1: From the Root

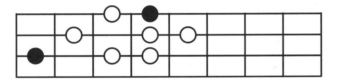

Form 2: From the Third

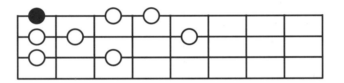

Form 3: From the Fifth

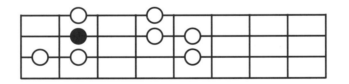

Form 4: Horizontal Form

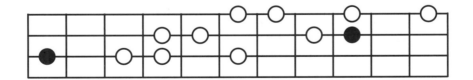

MELODIC MINOR

This scale can also be used over minor chords and is commonly referred to as the "jazz minor" scale.

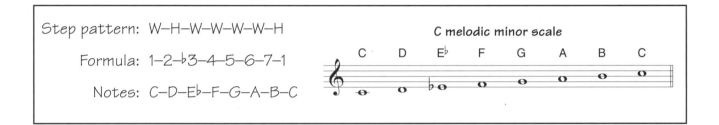

Step pattern: W–H–W–W–W–W–H

Formula: 1–2–♭3–4–5–6–7–1

Notes: C–D–E♭–F–G–A–B–C

C melodic minor scale

Form 1: From the Root

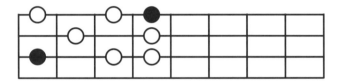

Form 2: From the Third

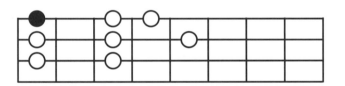

Form 3: From the Fifth

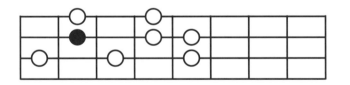

Form 4: Horizontal Form

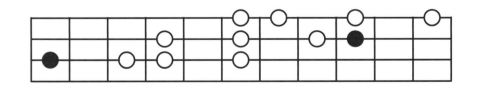

MINOR PENTATONIC

This is undeniably the most prevalent scale used by rock and blues players. As its name suggests ("penta" means five), this scale contains only five different tones.

Step pattern: W+H–W–W–W+H–W

Formula: 1–♭3–4–5–♭7–1

Notes: C–E♭–F–G–B♭–C

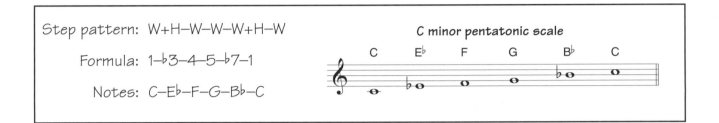

C minor pentatonic scale

Form 1: From the Root

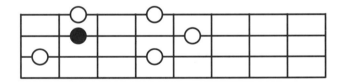

Form 2: From the Third

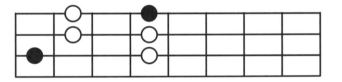

Form 3: From the Fifth

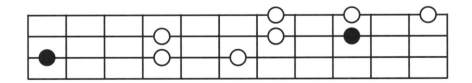

Form 4: Horizontal Form

MAJOR PENTATONIC

This is another five-tone ("pentatonic") scale common in many styles of music. It has a "bright" sound that lends itself well to country music.

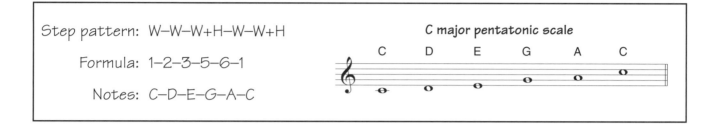

Step pattern: W–W–W+H–W–W+H

Formula: 1–2–3–5–6–1

Notes: C–D–E–G–A–C

C major pentatonic scale

Form 1: From the Root

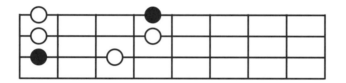

Form 2: From the Third

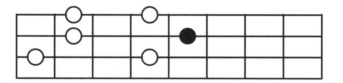

Form 3: From the Fifth

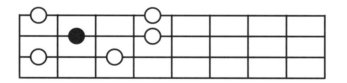

Form 4: Horizontal Form

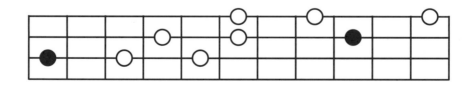

BLUES

The blues scale is common in jazz, rock, and (you guessed it!) blues music. It's like a minor pentatonic scale but with an added "blue" note (♭5), which makes it a six-tone scale.

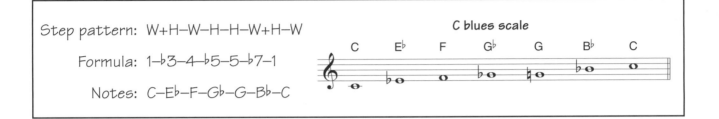

Step pattern: W+H–W–H–H–W+H–W

Formula: 1–♭3–4–♭5–5–♭7–1

Notes: C–E♭–F–G♭–G–B♭–C

C blues scale

C   E♭   F   G♭   G   B♭   C

Form 1: From the Root

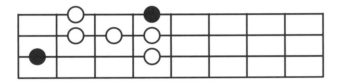

Form 2: From the Third

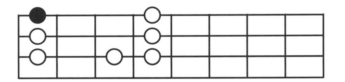

Form 3: From the Fifth

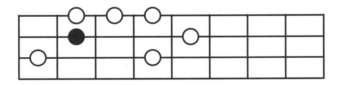

Form 4: Horizontal Form

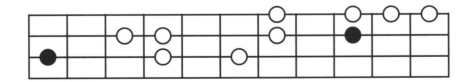

DIMINISHED

This scale is popular in jazz and heavy metal music (turn it up!). NOTE: It's not a typo; there really are eight different tones in this scale.

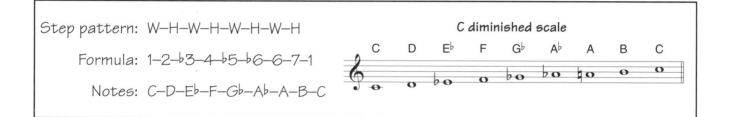

Step pattern: W–H–W–H–W–H–W–H

Formula: 1–2–♭3–4–♭5–♭6–6–7–1

Notes: C–D–E♭–F–G♭–A♭–A–B–C

C diminished scale

Form 1: From the Root

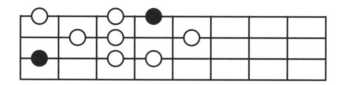

Form 2: From the Third

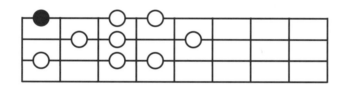

Form 3: From the Fifth

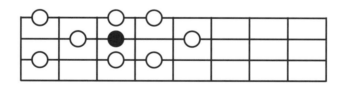

Form 4: Horizontal Form

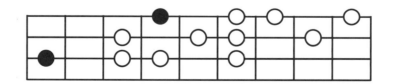

MODES

Modes are like scales—each uses a specific pattern of whole steps and half steps. The difference is that a mode is not related to the key of its root note. That is, a Dorian mode built on C is not in the key of C. The seven modes in common practice today are derived from the seven notes of the major scale: Ionian starts on the first (root) note and is therefore identical to the major scale, Dorian starts on the second, Phrygian starts on the third, etc.

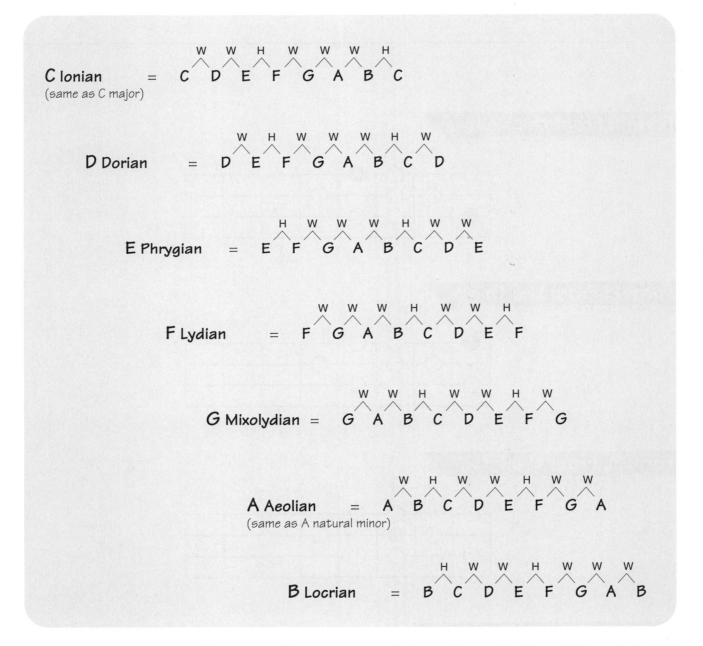

As you can see, each mode is actually a variation of the major scale. They differ only in the arrangement of the intervals.

The next page gives you two usable patterns for each of the seven modes—one starting on the root and the other starting on the fifth.

Ionian

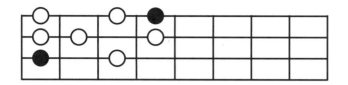 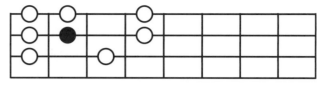

Dorian

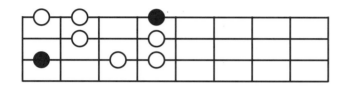 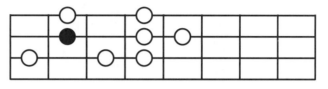

Phrygian

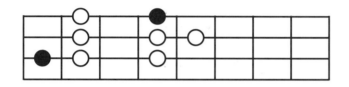 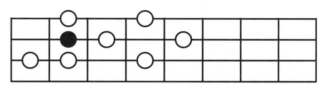

Lydian

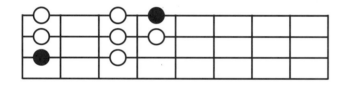 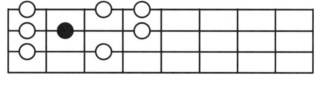

Mixolydian

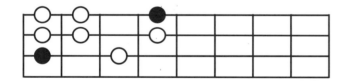 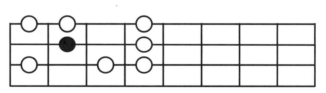

Aeolian

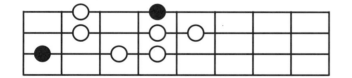 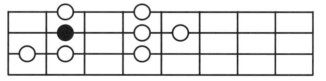

Locrian

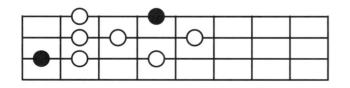 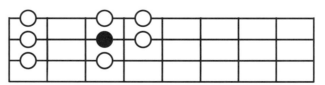

JAM SESSION

Time to charge admission...

Now it's time to use the chords and scales from this book and make some **actual music**! This section provides twenty chord progressions found in various music styles. Play along with the audio. You can either follow the chord symbols and strum along or use the suggested scales to practice improvising.

Either way, grab your axe, and let's jam!

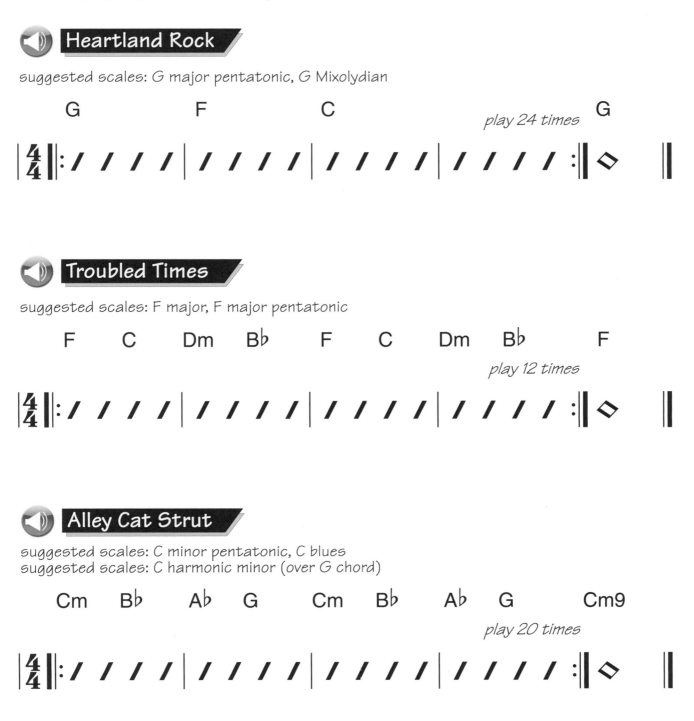

🔊 Heartland Rock

suggested scales: G major pentatonic, G Mixolydian

🔊 Troubled Times

suggested scales: F major, F major pentatonic

🔊 Alley Cat Strut

suggested scales: C minor pentatonic, C blues
suggested scales: C harmonic minor (over G chord)

Your Turn to Shuffle

suggested scales: C minor pentatonic, C blues

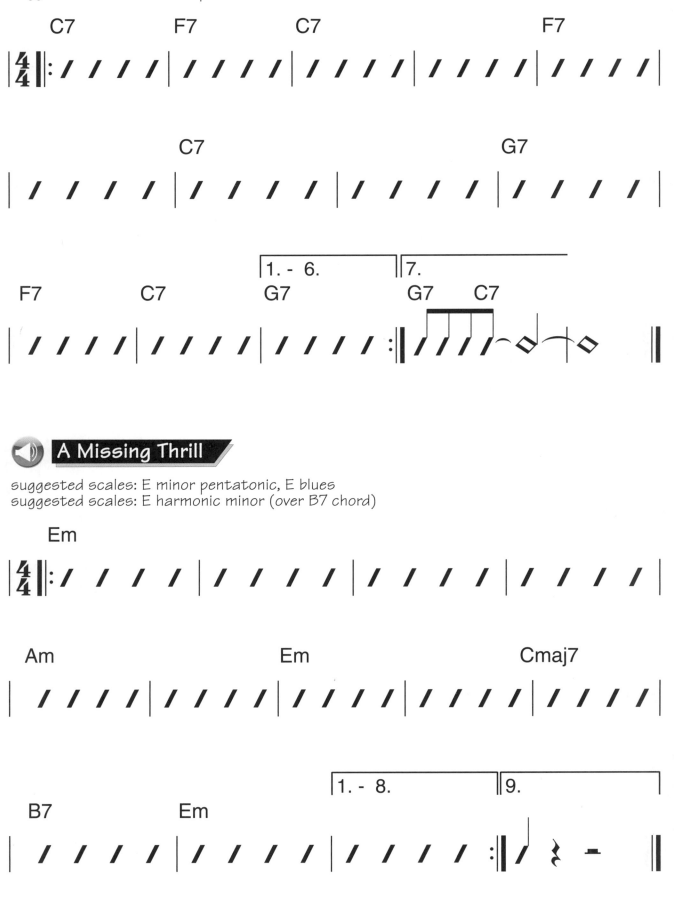

A Missing Thrill

suggested scales: E minor pentatonic, E blues
suggested scales: E harmonic minor (over B7 chord)

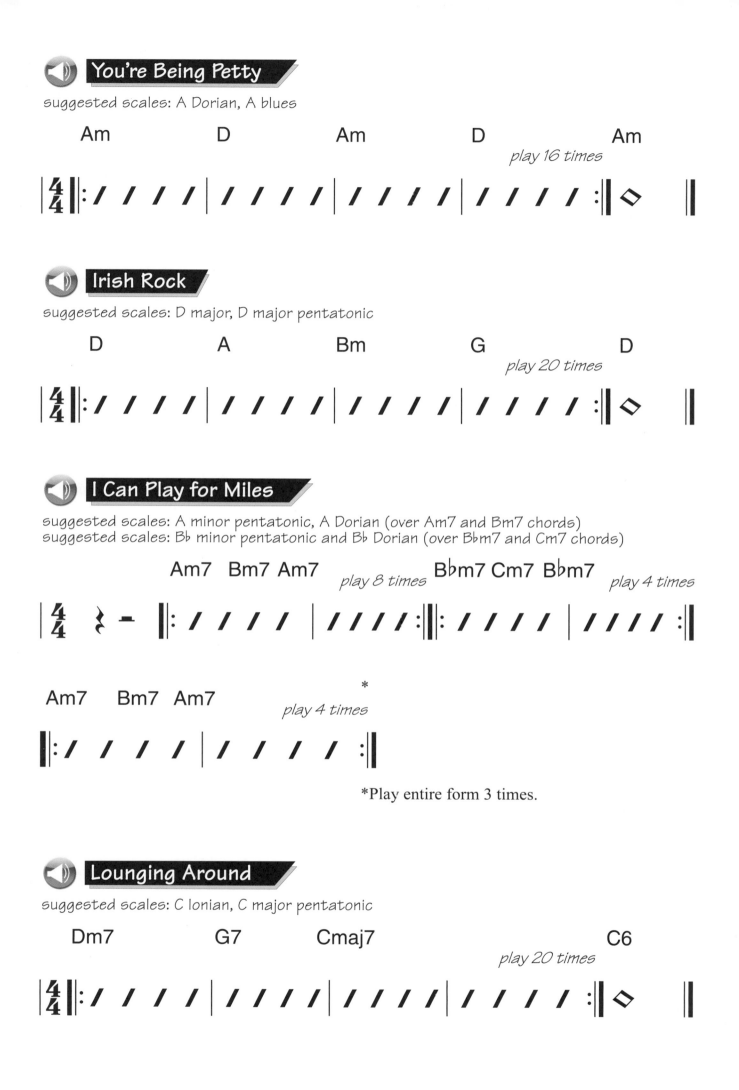

You're Being Petty

suggested scales: A Dorian, A blues

Irish Rock

suggested scales: D major, D major pentatonic

I Can Play for Miles

suggested scales: A minor pentatonic, A Dorian (over Am7 and Bm7 chords)
suggested scales: B♭ minor pentatonic and B♭ Dorian (over B♭m7 and Cm7 chords)

*Play entire form 3 times.

Lounging Around

suggested scales: C Ionian, C major pentatonic

Slow Minor Jam

suggested scales: D minor pentatonic, D blues
suggested scales: D harmonic minor (over A chord)

Dm   C   Bb   A   Dm

play 12 times

Lost in the Fifties

suggested scales: A major, A major pentatonic

A F#m   D   E   A F#m   D   E   A

play 12 times

Boots and Pickup Trucks

suggested scales: A major, A major pentatonic (over A and E7 chords)
suggested scales: B Mixolydian, B major pentatonic (over B7 chord)

A   B7

E7   A   A

play 10 times

Goin' to Church!

suggested scales: F major pentatonic, F blues, F Mixolydian

F   F

play 24 times

Garage Jam

suggested scales: G major pentatonic, G Mixolydian

Dreamy Rock

suggested scales: A minor, A minor pentatonic

City Lights

suggested scales: A major, A major pentatonic

Lydian Rock

suggested scales: A Lydian, A major pentatonic

*B chord over A bass note

🔊 Down and Dirty

suggested scales: G minor pentatonic, G blues

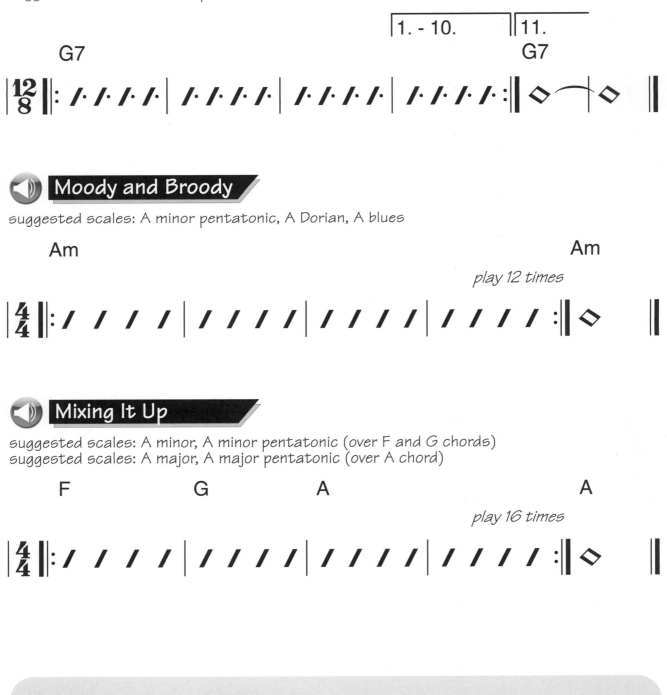

🔊 Moody and Broody

suggested scales: A minor pentatonic, A Dorian, A blues

🔊 Mixing It Up

suggested scales: A minor, A minor pentatonic (over F and G chords)
suggested scales: A major, A major pentatonic (over A chord)

☞ **Bravo!** You're ready for the big leagues...